D0475481

GHOST
HUNTING

GHOST HUNTING

A Survivor's Guide

JOHN FRASER

The
History
Press

This book is for Dominique, who forever raises my spirits.

First published 2010

The History Press
The Mill, Brimscombe Port
Stroud, Gloucestershire, GL5 2QG
www.thehistorypress.co.uk

British Library Cataloguing in Publication Data.
A catalogue record for this book is available from the British Library.

ISBN 978 0 7524 5414 6

Typesetting and origination by The History Press
Printed in India by Nutech Print Services

CONTENTS

ACKNOWLEDGEMENTS

Woodchester Manor Trust, for the photograph of Woodchester Manor; Philip Carr, for orbs and candle photographs; Ken MacKenzie, for the photograph of Ham House; Ann Bowker, for her photographs of Sandwood Bay; Eddie Brazil for his photographs of the Borley Rectory sie and Church; Rosemary Murdie, for all her assistance in drafting; and Dominique Fraser, for the photographs and for all her help and support.

INTRODUCTION

Hunting ghosts – science, pseudoscience or pastime?

Many people have a fascination for the unexplained. This may simply take the form of scaring oneself with novels or with films about the paranormal. One need only look at the success of such books as *Dracula* or *Frankenstein* in the nineteenth century, through to movies such as *The Exorcist* or, more recently, the most atmospheric film *The Others* to see that this appeal is timeless and perhaps innate in us all. For some, however, that interest goes a little deeper.

My own fascination began in the mid-1970s when I saw a then-rare television documentary on the subject called *The Ghost Hunters*. This featured Borley Rectory, renowned through much of the twentieth century as being the most haunted house in England. When I suddenly realised that people took such things seriously, the local library soon became mysteriously devoid of books on the subject as my fascination grew.

About a decade later, shortly after leaving university, I took the opportunity while up in Scotland to drive a barely roadworthy Vauxhall Viva up to the country's very north-east tip. My destination was a haunted place called Sandwood Cottage, a ruined shell of a former croft house at the desolate and also haunted Sandwood Bay. My mode of transport was of course entirely unsuitable for such a long trip. However, fate was on my side and the Automobile Association kindly replaced my gearbox as I stuttered through Perth, rather than tow me the 500 miles back to London. I was thus sent on my way, more through luck than judgement, to an active pursuit of my interest which has now lasted twenty years.

Sandwood Cottage was, and still is, perhaps the ultimate in ghost hunts. This is not because it is necessarily the most active, although it does have its fair share of sightings considering it is in the most desolate part of northern Scotland. Its 'ultimate' tag comes more because it is several miles from the nearest road, surrounded by peat bogs and reportedly quicksand. You are in effect trapped for the night in a haunted house! The cottage and bay is reportedly haunted by a bearded sailor, amongst other things. Whilst the nature of the haunting will be further discussed in later chapters, it is sufficient to say that this 'investigation' (especially after the loss of my high powered torch), was based on bravado rather than trying in any way to scientifically prove the paranormal. On arrival at dusk and discovering my lack of artificial light, I spent an initially nerve-racking but eventually very exhilarating night, without incident other than the unique feeling of creating an adventure into the unknown.

My research into the alleged haunting was thankfully far better organised than my rather amateur vigil and through swapping notes on the case with the writer Peter Underwood, I was invited to join the 'Ghost Club' of which he was then Chair. Subsequently, following far more experience, I spent a number of years as Vice Chair of the club, in charge of Investigations. Currently I am on the council of the Society for Psychical Research (SPR) whilst also co-ordinating investigations on their Spontaneous Case Committee.

My brief résumé about my entry into the subject is intended to show that most ghost hunters, including myself, start off with very little more than a thirst for adventure and an undirected urge to seek out the truth. As investigating the paranormal is by and large a voluntary, unpaid pastime, such motivations are of course essential. This does however lead to two key questions which perhaps form the essence of what this book is about:

Are such motivations sufficient to ensure that the paranormal can be investigated in such a way as to prove or disprove the phenomena?

🔖 *Can such evidence gathered from a ghost hunt be presented in a
scientific way to actually allow at least open-minded scientists to make
comment?*

When the first modern renaissance of paranormal investigation
came about in the mid to late nineteenth century, it was led to a
large extent by scientists at the forefront of their disciplines trying
to find a connection between their new scientific theories and the
unexplained phenomena of the age. The earlier presidents of the
SPR for example included:

🔖 *Balfour Stewart (1827-1887) – physicist; Professor of Physics at
Queens College, Manchester, from 1870; Fellow of the Royal Society.*

🔖 *Sir William Crookes (1832-1919) – chemist and physicist; discoverer of
thallium and cathode rays; inventor of radiometer.*

🔖 *Sir Oliver Lodge (1851-1940) – a renowned physicist.*

🔖 *Charles Richet (1850-1935) – French physiologist; Professor of
Physiology at the Faculty of Medicine of Paris; won the Nobel Prize
in 1913.*

It also included Arthur Balfour, who was president in 1893 and
who was also to become the Prime Minister at the turn of the
twentieth century. To put this in context, imagine David Cameron
being the president of a major paranormal investigation group. It
can be clearly seen then just how far the divide between paranormal investigations and society's leading scientists, academics and
public figures has become.

Through much of the twentieth century, although with perhaps
some recent exceptions, the standard bearers of the paranormal
have been independent-minded volunteers and, in a few cases,
professional authors. Both these categories have included the
insightful, the gullible and some who may have been simply
more interested in what sells books. While a few scientists have

remained involved, a fair percentage of those do so quite openly to debunk rather than to engage in open-minded research.

Perhaps because of this detachment by science, or perhaps because of the nature of the subject itself, real progress throughout the twentieth century was fairly minimal and normally controversial.

Is this a state of affairs which those who are interested in the subject should be comfortable with? If our only aim is to delve into the subject for our own satisfaction, with the same sense of adventure that took me up to a deserted cottage in a battered car in the middle of nowhere, then perhaps it presents no problems at all. This independent type of investigation flourishes today like never before, and can at times be practised to a very high standard. The late and sadly departed Maurice Grosse, a former colleague of mine in the SPR, had far more success in his first investigation. He was sent to look into a case that became famously known as the Enfield Poltergeist, and which became the subject of books and much media coverage. Yet even with such a well-documented and researched poltergeist case, it was not possible to engage outsiders from the mainstream scientific community to any great extent.

Ghost hunting and other types of paranormal investigation therefore have an ongoing problem – most of its participants are unsure in the longer term as to what they really hope to achieve. Moreover, as there are no generally accepted standards as to how to investigate, it is debatable how many investigators do it properly, even in the most basic sense. However, the enthusiasm and thirst for knowledge about the paranormal is at a level perhaps not seen since the First World War. The potential for good investigating and at least some real progress is undoubtedly there.

There have been hundreds of books written about ghosts and other types of paranormal phenomena, but relatively few have been written about how people investigate the phenomena and the subject itself. I would hope then that this book would work at two levels:

Firstly in providing ideas for good and productive investigations which can bring participants to some well thought out conclusions about what they have experienced.

Secondly, and of equal importance, by delving into the past, present and possible future of research as a whole, I would wish to provide some thoughts and resources that may assist all interested in the subject to co-operate more fully in their aims and discoveries.

I hope at these two levels it will be of interest both to beginners and those already a little more involved, as well as those with just a general passing interest. From my own background, most of my experience has come from investigating the existence of ghosts. The book will therefore tend to concentrate on this area, although any conclusions may well be applicable to investigating different types of phenomena.

Having stated that this book should work on two levels, I also have a desire that whatever practical and scientific advice that it gives, it should also seek to convey how fascinating, interesting and exciting investigating the unexplained can be. Most of us who have even the slightest interest in exploring the paranormal do it partly for the feeling of living a little on the edge (although in fact it is an incredibly safe interest to pursue). This has always been part of the tradition of the subject and it need not, and should not, be sanitised.

As with any book that tackles the investigation of the unexplained, it would be a contradiction to come up with any set-in-stone formula. I certainly do not have all the answers, but I would hope that what follows would give insight into the history of ghost hunting and some good current practices. In doing this it may also help to put together some of the pieces of this fascinating jigsaw of phenomena that still lie outside of science, but very much in the domain of the ghost hunter.

one

A Brief History of Ghost Hunting

Modern fad or ancient art?

Pliny the Younger recorded what has been regarded as the first story of a ghost hunt in AD 100. The anecdote concerns a haunted house in ancient Athens being investigated by a philosopher named Athenodoros Cananites. According to Pliny, the ghost would rattle chains and take the form of an old man with a beard, which shows perhaps how little our idea of what a ghost is has changed. Surprisingly, it may perhaps be this story that started the stereotypical image of a ghost in rattling chains as there are few, if any, other ghost reports that in any way reflect this stereotype. 'Grey' and 'White' ladies, monks and nuns apparently haunt in abundance, but a classical report from two millennia ago is perhaps the only reason for perceiving that ghosts come complete with noisy chains. This is an interesting observation in itself, and an example of a reoccurring theme in ghost hunting of mythology masquerading as fact, which we will be exploring throughout this book. Nevertheless, Pliny the Younger was a most respected historian of the time, and it is thus likely that as far back as 2,000 years ago there were unexplained phenomena which people of education were investigating in a serious way.

With the oncoming of Christianity as a religious force and its generally hostile attitude to physical manifestations of the paranormal, serious investigations were on the whole put on hold for the next one and a half millennia. Thus the medieval age only brought snippets of paranormal investigation, such as William of Newburgh, an Augustinian canon, who reported paranormal events in his twelfth-century chronicles. He describes a haunting in the north of England and Scotland, where dead men were believed to rise from their graves at night. Although William himself may have been more open-minded than most as to the cause of such apparent phenomena, they were seen by those locally and by many in the Church at the time as being demonic rather than a benign afterlife visitation. This type of attitude, culminating in the various witch-hunts that spread throughout Europe, would have made it very difficult for such phenomena to have been investigated in an objective way. As an aside, please also note that this fairly well-known historic case may well here have set another stereotype in motion, as there are virtually no recent reported cases of even 'alleged' entities emerging from their coffins. Yet as an image of a ghost, it is perhaps as famous as our equally rare man rattling his chains.

Perhaps the most famous of these 'investigators' working under the eye of a suspicious church was Dr John Dee (1527-1608), who, whilst both a gifted academic and astrologer, is perhaps best known as the first major figure to use mediums to facilitate 'paranormal' communications, whilst still generally staying in the favour of the numerous kings and queens that reigned through his long life.

However, the choice of mediums used in his work was perhaps not ideal. More than one of them ended up in prison and the most famous of them, an Irishman called Edward Kelly, was already without his ears as a punishment for forgery. Whilst many of the communicants made claims to be angels, the style of communications through Kelly was very much the same as a modern medium. There was certainly much to be said in any case for communicating with angels at a time when most other supernatural beings were associated with witchcraft and devil worship.

This odd couple (earless forger and gifted academic) managed to make quite an impact on several European courts. However, whilst Edward Kelly was never specifically caught cheating, the content of some of the messages to Dee were certainly indicative of a charlatan. This was especially so with the repeated communications by the angel 'Uriel' to Kelly, who urged that each man should share the other's wife. Dee was by then a fairly old man who had married a much younger wife. However, such a communication did not discredit Kelly in Dee's eyes, and such was his belief in the spirit communications that some actually think this paranormally-induced wife swap may have occurred. This is surely the first of many examples of an intelligent man involved in investigating the paranormal whose desire to believe overcame his desire to discover the objective truth. We will say more of this later, but this is a predisposition of many ghost hunters and paranormal researchers, and perhaps one of the reasons that it has been kept on the fringe throughout so much of its history.

The last witchcraft execution in England (of the unfortunate Alice Molland) took place in 1684 and witchcraft trials had largely disappeared by 1712. Whilst eighteenth-century society did then relax the view that most things paranormal were the work of evil spirits, this did not result in an immediate increase in paranormal research. For that we had to wait until well into the nineteenth century when, in the space of a few decades, a whole new outlook on investigating such things developed. This was also combined with either an upturn in phenomena or, perhaps more likely, the better recording of phenomena in publications.

One of the first, and yet now a lesser-known example of modern paranormal investigating, was by a certain Major Edward Moor. He both investigated and compiled accounts of true ghost stories in his book called *Bealings Bells*, which he published privately in 1841.

The book primarily concentrated on an outbreak of mysterious bell ringing (of the inner house servants' bells) in 1834 at Great Bealings House, at Great Bealings in Suffolk, the author's home. Due to the publicity subsequently gained, more well-corroborated accounts of similar bell ringing and other varied phenomena in houses throughout the country were passed on to the author via correspondence. These were also included in his book.

The author, a professional soldier, writer and scholar made no firm claims that the nature of the strange occurrences were proof of spirits or ghosts and was very level-headed in his approach. Convinced, however, from his experimentation that there was no normal cause for the bell ringing, he labelled it 'preternatural' or beyond the current understanding of science. He took care to explain the common-sense precautions he made to check for the possibility of trickery at a time when even orthodox scientific methodology was still very much in its developmental stage.

The well-documented secondhand accounts of very similar unaccountable bell ringing in other houses seem to make this a phenomenon of its time and show Moor had also researched the subject well. It is interesting to note that the famous ghost hunter, Harry Price, on one of his first visits to Borely Rectory described in his *Confessions of a Ghost Hunter*, heard a similar outbreak of bell ringing from disused rooms in the house. He then described the checks that he made on the mechanisms which, nearly a century later, sounded very nearly identical to those of the Major's. So whatever the truth, Major Moor's techniques and enquiries were undoubtedly sound for their time, giving us an early example of all the traits a good ghost hunter should have, long before this term was even properly invented. It was only a mere decade later that investigating ghosts and the paranormal started to take off as a respectable pursuit by scientists and the upper and academic classes.

Regardless of the truth or otherwise of their claims, it was three impoverished New York sisters that brought the investigation of ghosts and the paranormal to the attention of the nineteenth-century middle classes more than any others. The family home of Leah, Maggie and Katy Fox was, in the early part of 1848, disturbed by nightly thumping noises very reminiscent of what today we would describe as a typical poltergeist case. The bangs and rappings seemed gradually to take on an intelligent form, and were perhaps the first conveyor of that now tried and tested séance room communication technique of 'one rap for yes, two raps for no'. They claimed to be that of a murdered peddler, Charles Rosa, and he also claimed his remains were in the cellar. Tantalisingly, some bones, apparently human, were found there.

The growing interest in the paranormal at the time turned what was an interesting occurrence into a press feeding frenzy, which the Fox sisters took full advantage of by touring the country as a stage show. This alleviated their poverty and ensured they became comparable to a paranormal version of the 'Spice Girls'. (The clever use of press publicity propelled the Fox sisters to overnight stardom in much the same way as the 1990s 'Brit Pop' sensations.)

Where the Foxes had a greater lasting impact however, was in the number of copycat incidents that seemed to come from their fame. Séances in the way that the term is now popularly understood (groups sitting in circles led by a medium that would produce phenomena or messages from the dead) became widespread, and by 1855 it was reported that the new 'religion' of spiritualism, based around afterlife communications, had over 2 million members world-wide. Whilst the Fox sisters were to become mired in controversy (Maggie Fox herself claimed it was but a conjuring act involving the cracking of their toes, a confession she later recanted), the phenomena which they either discovered or manufactured had in the meantime taken on a life of its own.

In the United Kingdom, the Fox sisters also had a large impact, and the coming decades were to consolidate interest in the phenomena. Organisations were formed to promote this new phenomena-based religion. These included the Spiritualist Association of Great Britain, founded in 1872 and still thriving in its Belgravia premises today, and the council for Psychic Studies. This was set up in 1884 and specialised, amongst other things, in spiritual healing. There also emerged offshoots such as 'spiritism' (the spiritualist doctrine of after-life communication combined with a belief in reincarnation). These new organisations, combined with a growing number of famous and infamous mediums (by far the most credible was Daniel Dunglas Home, who worked in normal light, and was never exposed as fraudulent), meant that by the latter part of the nineteenth century there was much indeed to be investigated.

Meanwhile, mainstream science of the nineteenth century was very much in a state of flux, and discoveries were happening that blew open the existing pattern of beliefs and which, to a large extent, helped to make the investigation of the paranormal credible. These discoveries started what could be called the 'Science of the Unseen' – a whole series of scientific breakthroughs during the century bringing science beyond traditional mechanics and direct cause and effect observation.

Below is a short summary of such discoveries:

- *1825 – British inventor William Sturgeon discovered electromagnetism, showing an astonished world how 9lb of metal could be lifted with a 7oz piece of electrically charged iron.*

- *1831 – The discovery of electromagnetic induction quickly followed when Michael Faraday managed to convert magnetism into electricity by moving a magnet through a coil of wire. On this, the foundations of practical electronic generation was built.*

- *1837 – British physicist William Cooke, along with Charles Wheatstone, invented the electrical version of the telegraph using these newly-discovered principles of electromagnetism.*

- *1865 – Radio waves were being mathematically predicted by Scottish mathematician James Clerk Maxwell, who saw the similarity between the wave-like properties of light and electromagnetism.*

- *1875 – Alexander Graham Bell and Thomas Watson had adapted the principles behind the telegraph to facilitate the transmission of speech, ultimately becoming the telephone.*

- *1887 – The Serbian inventor and genius Tesla (who was described by his biographer, Robert Lomas, as 'the man who invented the twentieth century') discovered a system for alternating current generation.*

- *1893 – Tesla also took Maxwell's predictions further by transmitting radio waves. Further transmissions were made independently by the British scientist Oliver Lodge in 1894 and again in 1895 by the Italian, Marconi. Marconi used the practical applications of radio waves to well-known effect and very much became known as the father of radio communication.*

- *1905 – Einstein makes his first presentations on his theory of relativity.*

With the discovery of such a number of interrelated unseen forces and the revolutionary effects they could have on people's lives, it was perhaps not at all surprising that many wondered whether it was possible to actually discover the true nature of the paranormal. Perhaps it was just another unseen, undiscovered force? Indeed, two of the scientists I have mentioned above very much dabbled in the paranormal. Oliver Lodge was an early Chair of the Society of Psychical Research, while Tesla theorised about the occult to such an extent that his reputation suffered at least some temporary damage. None the less, it was probably from this 'science of the unseen' that the practical investigation of the paranormal, by those other than just theologians and alchemists, became an interesting possibility and has remained so to this day.

There was thus a desire and need amongst the educated classes to explore the unexplained, and spiritualism in particular, at this time. It may have in fact been the antics of the Davenport brothers, two particularly successful mediums or conjurers (depending on your outlook) from America, that provoked an array of 'gentlemen investigators' to join together in 1862 and form the Ghost Club. This lays claims to be the world's oldest organisation that still investigates the paranormal. Its early members may well have included Charles Dickens, as well as such dignitaries as A.H. Gordon, the then Lieutenant-Governor of New Brunswick.

The Ghost Club relaunched itself in 1882, and has had a long and successful history. Unlike the major spiritualist societies, and the Society for Psychical Research which was also set up in 1882, it never took the opportunity to purchase its own accommodation in the then slightly more modest parts of London such as Belgravia or Kensington. This lack of real estate investment unfortunately has kept the club in a financial position where it can only be run by hardworking volunteers, rather than paid staff.

With the coming of the Ghost Club and the SPR, ghost hunting and paranormal investigation at last had respectable and official bodies to oversee them. What also started to occur was the publication of mainstream books on the subject. Two of the better efforts of the period were *Ghost World*, written in 1893 by the Reverend T.F. Thiselton-Dyer, and a publication in 1907 with the no-nonsense title of *Haunted Houses* by Charles G. Harper.

Thiselton-Dyer's book is an interesting pot-pourri of cases, interspersed with theories of the time. These include an intriguing theory that ghosts may not cross water. The evidence he gives includes a fascinating tale of a certain Sergeant Munro of the Highland Police burying a murder victim's boots underwater in an attempt to lay, or trap, his ghost. (Surely not putting the needs of the victim first!)

Much emphasis was also placed on theories of hauntings being caused by those who had been buried without proper religious rites. He uses this as a plausible explanation as to why castles and old homes which are often sites of battles and murders might be more haunted than a 'modern' flat. This predominance of hauntings around such places is still a phenomena that is provoking new theories today.

Harper's book was very much in the 'gazetteer of haunted places' style, with which any ghost hunter of today would be familiar. Also familiar are the actual cases themselves. Anyone who has read recent gazetteers will have heard of the Screaming Skull of Bettiscombe Manor, Catherine Howard's ghost at Hampton Court and the haunting at Ham House (where I was part of an investigation just a few years ago). It is fascinating to see that

these cases are also given prominence at the turn of the twentieth century. This could be an indication of strong well-evidenced
hauntings over a long period. It could also though be an indication
of the fact that many writers find the need to rely on old publications rather than original research in deciding whether a place is
to be categorised as haunted. (As a ghost hunter it is essential to
discover which of these categories your 'haunted' site falls into.)

Whilst both Thiselton-Dyer and Harper wrote good books on
ghosts, neither could in any way be called a specialist writer of
the genre, let alone a ghost hunter. Thistleton-Dyer's other publications included *British Customs: Past and Present, The Folklore of
Plants* and *Royalty in All Ages*. Harper was basically a travel writer
whose other numerous publications included *The Old Inns of
England, The North Devon Coast* and what must have been a fascinating 1910 publication called *The Autocar Road Book*. However,
the first true professional ghost hunter was hot on their heels in
the shape of the prolific writer Elliott O'Donnell (1872-1965).

O'Donnell's publications on ghosts covered half a century from
Some Haunted Houses, which was published in 1908, through to
Haunted Waters, and Trees of Ghostly Dread (1958). To leave us in no
doubt as to what he considered himself to be, other titles included
Twenty Years' Experience as a Ghost Hunter (1916) and *Confessions of
a Ghost Hunter* (1928).

Whilst making claims as the first self-styled ghost hunter,
O'Donnell was by all accounts a colourful figure who claimed
descent from Niall of the Nine Hostages, a character of Irish folklore of a similar stature to Britain's King Arthur. As a young man
he claimed to have had a Dublin phantom attempt to strangle
him which considering the generally safe nature of ghost hunting as a pursuit, can be seen either as most unlucky or as a touch
of whimsy. He drifted through jobs, working as a cowboy on the
Oregon range, a policeman during the crushing of the infamous
Chicago Rail Strike (where police and army killed up to thirty-
five strikers), and then back in England as a schoolmaster.

His first attempts at writing, perhaps tellingly, were fiction, including a psychological thriller titled *For Satan's Sake*,

published in 1904. He soon found his niche in factual tales of the supernatural, of which he published round about forty books in a very readable (not to be read at the dead of night by candle-light) style.

He may have been the first (and was certainly not the last) ghost hunter with a touch of the showman about him and we should not necessarily discount him for that. What does discount his work as being of much use to serious researchers is the exten-sive use of anonymity in the locations which preclude further investigation and make it impossible to check authenticity.

A short extract from Chapter Two of his book *Animal Ghosts* shows both the very readable style in which he wrote and the way he would never make it easy for the reader to find the loca-tion of the event:

> A house in Birmingham near the Roman Catholic Cathedral was once
> very badly haunted... On one occasion the tenant's wife, on entering
> the sitting room was almost startled out of her senses at seeing a stout
> man with a large grey dog by his side. What was so alarming about
> the man was his face – it was apparently a mere blob of flesh without
> features in it.

One could attribute the anonymity to the gentlemanly style of writing of the times and a wish not to embarrass anyone with ghost stories relating to their premises. However, even Reverend Thiselton-Dyer, a good man of the cloth, does not seem to be quite so restrained in this respect. Charles Harper goes even further, identifying all his haunted sites without any real hesita-tion. He even draws an illustration and gives directions to get to 'Hillside', a haunted private dwelling in suburban Egham. (Perhaps in this instance the owners may have preferred Elliott O'Donnell's more vague and whimsical approach.)

Sadly then, whilst O'Donnell was a prolific and entertaining writer, it is impossible to call him a true ghost hunter in the way that we understand it today as his publications left little in the way of solid fact for future investigators to check. For the type of ghost hunter and writer that we take so much for granted today, we must move much further into the twentieth century and the equally colourful figure of Harry Price.

There have perhaps been more books written about Harry Price (1881-1948), his exaggerated claims and accusations that he fabricated phenomena than he ever wrote himself about ghosts. Indeed, Price is the only paranormal investigator to my knowledge with the unique accusation against him of faking a photograph showing false mediumship. This happened in his investigation into the medium Rudi Schneider, when supporters of the medium accused Price of doctoring a photograph which appeared to show Schneider's hand moving freely at a time when it should have been restrained.

Price came to fame in the 1920s and '30s, initially through his investigation into physical mediums such as Stella Cranshaw, Eileen Garrett and the Schneider brothers (as mentioned previously). This was but a warm-up for the publicity generated by his investigations into the haunting of the now-renowned Borley Rectory, which led to his two best-selling books with the understated titles *The Most Haunted House in England* (1940) and *The End Of Borley Rectory* (1946).

However, any summary on the character flaws of Price and whether they influenced the results of his investigations would take far too long to fit into this brief history of ghost hunting, and would perhaps be irrelevant to it. In my opinion, the ultimate contribution that Harry Price made to the subject was not in how he may or may not have actually carried out his investigations, but in the objective and scientific way that he proposed that investigations should be carried out.

Price opened his National Laboratory of Psychical Research at the start of 1926, and it quickly became a credible rival to the SPR. As with most things Price did, it generated a media frenzy. However, it did boast some much respected parapsychologists from around the world amongst its members. These included Schrenck-Notzing of Munich, Eugene Osty of Paris, Fritz Grunewald of Berlin and Christian Winther of Copenhagen.

The equipment used in the laboratory was based on the principles of electrical engineering and included such fascinating names as the custom-built telekintoscope. Whilst no details as to the working of this painful sounding device are now readily available, the general thrust of such equipment was to use the technology of the day to provide suitable controls for the testing of mediums and others with apparent paranormal abilities. Other, more established, equipment to this effect included:

- *Electroscopes – used to detect the presence and magnitude of electric charge on a body.*

- *Galvanometers – used for detecting and measuring electric current.*

- *Barographs – a now antiquated piece of equipment used to make a continuous recording of atmospheric pressure, in effect a barometer with a 'pen arm'.*

- *Thermographs – used to make continuous readings of temperature. As with a barograph this was in effect a thermometer with a 'Pen Arm'.*

- *Air testers – used for recording the circulation of the air.*

- *Min/max thermometers – in effect a 'poor man's' thermograph with the ability only to measure the highest and lowest temperature over a period. However, these devices were far more portable and easier to set up.*

The laboratory also boasted a photographic studio, a library and an isolation chamber for testing telekinetic phenomena, leaving Mr Price better equipped than all but the most sophisticated ghost hunters of today. Whilst the array of equipment is most impressive and took paranormal investigation to a new level, I can't help but wonder what 'theory' of the paranormal much of this equipment was testing for. How would a barograph, for example (primarily used to test air pressure for weather forecasting), disprove or quantify the supernatural? Ghosts are surely not just 'fair weather' friends. There was, after all, no real working hypothesis amongst ghost hunters of the time that air pressure in any way affected paranormal phenomena. Was the use of such equipment then simply to create the impression that the investigation was scientific and high-tech? I mention this as the overuse or misuse of advanced technological equipment is something that we may still be guilty of today. That being said however, during the 1930s the level of activity and interesting results that came from Price were most impressive. Whether he always kept to his own standards of investigation or not, the standards that he publicly promoted were perhaps not met by others for at least another half-century.

Price's other main piece of foresight was in his efforts to connect up with the mainstream scientific community by way of reorganising his laboratory as the London University Council for Psychical Investigation. Whilst not quite a formal part of the London University, it was a project assisted by a good number of its academics and was certainly the first effort in this country to formally link paranormal research with mainstream science. A more formal offer was to come in 1937, when the University of Bonn in Germany was to offer Price the chance of setting up a department of parapsychology. Bearing in mind there was already a Nazi government in place (and the Second World War was but two years away) it was perhaps either a credit to Price's judgement, or possibly just plain good luck, that he did not take up this appointment.

Harry Price has been characterised as a paper bag salesman who supplemented his income by posing as an expert in psychic phenomena. However, I think this rather misses the point. Most paranormal investigators were, or still are, involved in another form of employment. Harry Price was indeed in the paper bag industry, so to make this a criticism is surely a type of intellectual snobbery. That he ultimately made a good living from the paranormal is undoubtedly true, but why should paranormal investigators be poverty stricken and penniless? In most other areas of life, including scientific disciplines, a good salary would be an indication of success. Price has also been criticised for some of his case choices, including investigating a talking mongoose on the Isle of Man or spending the night (fully-clothed, of course, in those conservative times) in a haunted bed in Chiswick Museum with his colleague, Professor Joad. Regarding these cases though, who is to really say when a reported paranormal phenomenon is too paranormal to investigate? Remember, if just for a minute we accept current scientific theories as being complete and correct, all paranormal phenomena starts to sound pretty silly. If there is some evidence that a bed is haunted, then it needs investigating. If it generates interest or even amusement by some, then so be it.

In short, Harry Price was a dammed good, groundbreaking investigator, who may or may not have been tempted at times to fake phenomena. In either case, he was pivotal in both popularising and progressing ghost hunting and other types of paranormal investigations.

After the death of Harry Price in 1948, ghost hunting seemed to enter a temporary lull. He was indeed a hard act to follow. In addition, even though the Second World War was over, Britain was still going through a period of austerity, and the quaint pastime of ghost hunting must have been seen as something of an unnecessary luxury. Price's National Laboratory ceased to exist, and whilst the SPR continued to function, it was perhaps not in as high a profile a way as it had done in either the Victorian period or in the 1930s. The Ghost Club, which had been relaunched by Harry Price in 1936, again ceased activities for a number of years.

This lull was perhaps partly due to the falling off of the number of effective physical mediums, which had to some extent been the bread and butter of most paranormal investigators. (After all, people who claim they can summon up phenomena at will are far easier to test than places where phenomena may occur from time to time). Physical mediums that were still active were perhaps less willing to be tested after the number of exposés in the 1930s by Harry Price and others. Mediums were given further reasons to be nervous of public testing after one of their more famous practitioners, Helen Duncan, was ridiculously prosecuted in 1943 – at the Old Bailey no less. She was charged with conspiracy to con-travene the ancient and, until then, long-buried Witchcraft Act of 1735! Worse still was the fact she was found guilty. Whilst not receiving the same fate as the hapless Alice Molland (the last witch to be executed), Duncan did receive the seemingly harsh sentence of nine months in prison.

For all these reasons, the times when a paranormal investigator could easily bring physical phenomena to be tested in a place of his choice by using a 'gifted' physical medium had passed. Over the next two decades, this was gradually replaced by field research based around haunted buildings or sites. Thus it was perhaps through necessity that site-based ghost hunting evolved to what it is today.

There was yet another successful rebirth of the Ghost Club in 1955. (It seems this particular club in itself gives proof of reincar-nation.) Peter Underwood became its president in 1960, having been one of the last members invited to join by Price before his death in 1948.

Within a decade, Peter Underwood had also become a successful author as well as the Ghost Club President. He published a string of ghost hunting books that caught the public's imagination, espe-cially so the gazetteer style of publication which seemed to show the public that there was a haunted site literally around the corner from their own homes. Such publications included *A Gazetteer of British Ghosts* (1971), *A Gazetteer of Scottish and Irish Ghosts* (1973) and *Haunted Wales* (1978). He also produced many more general books on the subject, such as his *Dictionary of the Supernatural* (1978).

Underwood's books were well written and very readable, and ensured that the public had for the first time an easily accessible and locatable reference to the UK's most haunted sites. Like Harry Price, he also managed to leave his day job at a publishing house and become one of that very rare breed of 'professional' ghost hunters. Though now well into his ninth decade, he continues to write and publish.

However, Peter Underwood was by no means the only key ghost hunter of the 1970s. The late Andrew Green (1927-2004) took the sensible stance that if the public were to be informed about their haunted places, the places reported on should at least have been haunted in living memory. His comprehensive and fascinating volume *Our Haunted Kingdom* (1973) excluded any site if there had not been a credible report in the last twenty-five years. As we will see later, this unfortunately excludes a huge number of famous 'allegedly' haunted places, which rather makes the important point that ghost stories can also have an afterlife long beyond that of the ghost itself. Green was also the first to publish a book about the process of ghost hunting itself in his *Ghost Hunting: A Practical Guide* (1976). Underwood in turn brought his expertise on the subject to the public domain with his own book, *The Ghost Hunter's Guide* (1986). It is interesting to read these books and see just how approaches to ghost hunting have changed over the last thirty years.

Also of note during this renaissance of ghost hunting books was Mark Alexander, a former journalist who found a fascination in the subject and used his writing skills to produce a trilogy of extremely readable books (*Haunted Castles*, *Phantom Britain* and *Haunted Inns*). A contemporary *Sunday Times* review on one of his books stated that it 'oozes with history and atmosphere', and it is indeed true that his books manage to convey his material as a good ghost story. However, he managed to do this without losing the factual content, and without using the whimsy that Elliott O'Donnell reverted to in order to entertain.

One of the many other contributions worth a mention is what I believe was the first travel atlas-style guide to ghosts; the lusciously produced and wonderfully photographed *Haunted Britain* (1973) by Anthony Hippisley Coxe. The book only gives the briefest of notes on each site and probably added little to the ghost hunting debate. However, it had an uncanny ability to make you want to get out into a car and travel to every one of the places mentioned. Thus, for no other reason than its success in enthusing future ghost hunters (such as myself), it is more than worthy of a mention.

Strangely though, whilst people were avidly reading about haunted places and ghost hunting, very few people were actually doing it. These books were in some way the equivalent of one of the glossy 'house and home' magazines where you love looking at the expensive furniture which you deep down know there is little chance you could ever buy. Unless you were fortunate enough to be invited to join the Ghost Club (which luckily I later was) or the few other well-established organisations, it was unlikely that any location would have then taken an *ad hoc* group of ghost hunters seriously.

Things opened up a bit in the 1980s, especially with the formation of the the Association for the Scientific Study of Anomalous Phenomena (ASSAP). Those who set it up saw it as a more inclusive alternative to the SPR, and it certainly brought new and enthusiastic people into investigating the paranormal. The 1980s also brought the publicising of a haunting which at least approached the magnitude and publicity of Borley Rectory in the 1930s. This case was very much a haunting of its time, that of a fairly modern council house in North London which became known as the 'Enfield Poltergeist', and which had intense activity for well over a year. The recorded phenomena included ghostly voices, levitation, wall writings and all manner of artefacts being thrown around the house. As you may recall from the introduction, this was actually the first case of my late and highly regarded SPR colleague Maurice Grosse. Despite being thrown in very much at the deep end, Maurice, with the assistance of the author Guy Playfair, managed to produce the most documented and publicised British investigation for a generation. Summarised by Guy Playfair's best-selling book, *This House Is Haunted*, the 'Enfield Poltergeist' case added a great deal of credibility to the subject and encouraged others to become more active in the field.

By the 1990s, with the popularisation of the subject through a wide selection of television shows such as Living TVs *Most Haunted*, ghost hunting became a seriously widespread interest. It now extended well beyond the pioneers, academics and eccentrics of the past 2,000 years, which I have briefly mentioned in this chapter. Clubs today are spread the length and breadth of Britain; from the quaintly named 'Mostghosts' ghost hunters of Cornwall through to the more plainly named 'Caithness Ghost Hunters' at Scotland's northern tip.

Does the inclusion of more people and more ghost hunts mean that there is more chance of finding evidence for a ghost, or are investigations too disparate and run on individualistic lines to be anything other than just an interesting experience for those who participate in them? Unfortunately, in many cases the latter is often true, which is why thirty years after Andrew Green published the first practical guide for ghost hunters in Britain, it is perhaps high time to both debate and update the conclusions that he and others reached.

I hope the coming chapters will make some contribution to this.

two

THE STATE OF GHOST HUNTING TODAY

Do quantity and quality go easily hand in hand?

There has been quite simply an explosion of interest recently in all aspects of the supernatural. If you look, for example, at the selection of channels on an average television package, you could quite easily spend half your evening watching programmes on the subject. Some make efforts to treat the subject intelligently whilst, of course, still seeking to entertain. Others are less ambitious in their aims. I was once asked by a television production company who should have know better, whether I would be willing to fake phenomena for a proposed show. I was happy to decline this offer. Thankfully, I do not believe that this show ever made the airwaves.

This explosion of interest is not just in the media. Most towns that have any semblance of a tourist industry now have a ghost walk of some sort or another, often run by ghost hunters themselves. The Chair of the Ghost Club, Alan Murdie, runs a very good example in Cambridge, while the current Events Officer, Philip Hutchinson (an actor by profession), has had a similar impact in Guildford. In some historic towns such as York, things have gone further still, with its haunted heritage becoming a key part of its official tourism industry. To quote the Visit York tourist website:

York – with its history of conflict and many tragic events – boasts
more than its fair share of ghoulies, ghosties and things that go bump
in the night. In fact, York claims to be Europe's most haunted city, and
sometimes it seems as though a ghostly figure with a score to settle is in
residence in just about every street or ginnel in town.

In fact, York has several competing ghost walks, as well as a ghost
cruise and other related activities.

Investigating the paranormal has, as a consequence of the above,
also become quite a boom industry. This could reflect the desire
of many to be entertained through an element of fear (a kind
of thinking-man's 'white knuckle' ride). It also surely reflects a
deeper, genuine interest in the subject by an ever larger group of
enthusiasts. As mentioned in the previous chapter, it is likely that
if you live in any reasonable-sized town, there will be some kind
of group or body involved in investigating the paranormal. There
is thus ever more opportunity to make practical use of a guide on
ghost hunting such as this.

The downside, however, is that with such an array of organisations it is perhaps all the more difficult to agree on an established
good practice. Some groups are dominated by those who are
out-and-out believers and are uncritical in their approach. Some,
such as the well-known organisation 'Skeptics in the Pub', would
perhaps have an instinctive tendency to believe that the only type
of spirits that exist are ones that they might purchase at the bar
during their meetings. A few organisations even charge the vul-
nerable to rid them of their entities. This practice is, of course, to
be deplored. Whilst the vast majority of organisations are surely
comprised of people with genuine motives and enquiring minds,
who aim to act as 'seekers of truth', there is of course no formally
accepted qualification in paranormal investigating. So even within
this group of people there is a vast difference in the effectiveness
in the way in which that 'truth' is actually sought.

There are actually three distinct types of bodies involved in
actively investigating the supernatural. These are:

- The long-established national groups, which are few in number.

- The local volunteer groups, of which I have just made brief mention.

- Finally, there are a small number of university departments in the UK which, over the last two decades, have actively and publicly participated in research. I will speak of these university groups separately in the next chapter.

This chapter and the next will explain, amongst other things:

- *How each of these types of bodies function.*

- *How they have evolved.*

- *Their possible strengths and weaknesses.*

- *The extent to which they interact with each other.*

- *What someone hoping to be further involved would gain from them.*

Let us first look at what I have called the long-established 'national groups', which are already slightly familiar to us, having had a key role in the history of the subject as summarised in the first chapter. There are only three organisations which I feel fit truly into this category. These are the Ghost Club, the Society for Psychical Research (SPR), and the Association for the Scientific Study of Anomalous Phenomena (ASSAP).

THE GHOST CLUB
Perhaps of the above three groups, the Ghost Club has the most instinctive appeal to those who are interested in ghost hunting. Although it does cover some other paranormal topics, the tradition of the Ghost Club has always predominantely followed that

of its title, to investigate the existence or otherwise of ghosts, poltergeists and other closely related phenomena.

From the 1960s to the 1990s, the Ghost Club was very closely associated with the paranormal author Peter Underwood, who was president throughout that time. It was at that period a club to join 'by invitation only' but for those who were invited, it was one of the few organisations which would actively seek out interesting sites to investigate. It also had a good programme of speakers on the subject. Peter Underwood's 1994 book, *Nights in Haunted Houses,* perhaps best sums up the activity of that period. He describes investigations in such high profile haunted sites as Glamis Castle, Chingle Hall, the Mermaid Inn (Rye) and Berry Pomeroy Castle. He also kindly takes a few pages to make mention of my efforts in investigation and research at Sandwood Bay, referred to in the introduction to this book.

However, in 1993, the entire nature of the Ghost Club was to change when an internal disagreement on the council led to Peter Underwood's resignation as president and his setting up of a rival organisation, the Ghost Club Society, taking approximately half of the membership with it.

The Ghost Club Society continued with valid ghost hunting events and projects for at least the next decade having taken with it some very key members, but it is the continuing Ghost Club itself that is now of most interest to budding researchers. A temporary shortage of members, combined with a desire to be more accessible, led to a much more open door policy for membership. The only hurdles to overcome now for one wishing to join the club is the deliberately long application form, which simply sifts out those who are not willing to spend an hour explaining their valid reasons for becoming a members.

By the end of the 1990s the Ghost Club had almost completely reinvented itself. From being a club that had a tendency to have slightly older members, it now encompassed all age ranges. Nearly all of the council, including the Chairman, Alan Murdie, were recruits from after the 'split'. I, as Vice Chair at the time, and the energetic Ghost Club stalwart Keith Morbey were the only two council members who were in the club under the Presidency of Peter Underwood. Thus in my mid-thirties, I could joke about being a club veteran.

What though does the revamped Ghost Club actually do, and is it something that should interest those that wish to learn about and participate in investigations?

The club's unique angle is that it remains part social, part educational and part investigative. The membership fee covers most events, including a comprehensive speakers' programme currently based around the Victory Services Club in central London. Great care has been taken over the last fifteen years to remind new members that there is every opportunity after formal business to retire to the bar and really get to know others of a like mind. In addition, it has a lively Christmas party, often a summer social event, a well-presented quarterly newsletter and an excellent website.

Investigations became more frequent during the latter part of the 1990s and are even more numerous today. Like most 'national' organisations, there is a slight tendency towards activities in the south-east. This tendency is not an excessive one however, partly due to the tireless efforts of Scottish-based member Derek Green, who has recently been appointed Investigations Officer, after single-handedly running a succession of high profile, well-documented investigations north of the border. At the turn of the millennium, the club also extended its activities internationally. Such activities included making contact and visiting Romanian parapsychologists and Dracula folklorists. Despite the fact that membership has trebled over the last fifteen years, it is thus fair to say that if you join the Ghost Club to ghost hunt there is every chance that you will be participating sooner rather than later.

Here, however, an interesting debate occurs. Can excessive inclusiveness in investigations rather kill off the 'goose that lays the golden egg' (the golden egg in this case being good quality evidence of the paranormal)?

Over the last few years, for example, the policy of the club has been to decide participation in investigations by lottery. Whilst this is logically speaking the fairest way to hold an 'event', there is a fairly strong possibility that it may result in an unbalanced investigations team. It could, for example, result in a team who are quite simply inexperienced in investigations and the interpretation of results. The newcomers would expect an element of guidance, which would not necessarily be there, and results could suffer accordingly. Just as threatening to the viability of an investigation is the scenario that throws up a team of investigators who quite simply do not know each other very well. An investigations organiser is then under threat of becoming an 'events organiser' trying to ensure everyone gets to know each other, so as not to be left with participants leaving investigation reports such as:

> On returning to base a shadowy apparition seemed to pass by in the corridor. The nice young lady in the blue sweatshirt (who I just met this evening) thought she had seen something too, although the tall middle aged sceptical guy (who I spoke to briefly at the Christmas party) thought it was just the moon passing behind clouds

Now that particular quote is pure fiction, but anyone who has tried to organise up to twenty people, many of them unknown to each other, will realise that it takes a great deal of concentration and effort. In the case of a paranormal investigation an organiser's concentration and effort is really needed in observation and ensuring the smooth running of any experimentation, rather than acting as a host or hostess to relative strangers.

However, I do not mean to be over-critical of the club's investigations. Even taking into account the things I have mentioned, they are of a fairly high standard. They also retain a good balance between old and new investigative techniques. Particularly successful recently have been what I call their 'investigations projects'. These are a series of repeat investigations in the same location, two of note being Michelin Priory in Sussex and Ham House in Richmond, Surrey. These have been run most effectively with the assistance of the then Press Office, Rosemary Murdie, and former Chair, Kathy Gearing. However, a key part of this book will be about trying to discover what makes a successful investigation, and thus the techniques of a club as long-standing as this have to be debated and analysed.

One further point worth mentioning is that whilst remarkable effort is made to be an inclusive club for its members, the club has a tendency to be not quite as open and inclusive with other, similar organisations. It tends not to share evidence very often or to take part in joint events. As some interesting anomalies have occurred over the years in Ghost Club investigations, it is a shame when they are not scrutinised further by their peers.

The Ghost Club has become a very good organisation for those with a passion for learning about, talking about and investigating the paranormal. If you are of such an inclination, you could do a lot worse than investing an hour of your time completing the application form. The club may not currently function to prove or disprove a type of phenomena to the outside world, but I have seen a number of members whose belief patterns have been altered after experiences in Ghost Club investigations. This is, assuming the evidence has been correctly interpreted, certainly an achievement in itself.

THE SPR

The Society for Psychical Research (SPR) is altogether a very different and more formal type of organisation. It was set up, like the Ghost Club, in the first mass wave of paranormal investigation in the Victorian age. Should one take into account the number of times the Ghost Club has temporarily folded and relaunched, it is probably the longest running organisation of this type. The SPR also, through luck, foresight or possibly even psychic judgement bought property in central London, whilst the Ghost Club was run through the hospitality of a series of London clubs. This has largely ensured it has had the ability to keep things on a professional rather than voluntary level, currently with one full-time and one part-time member of staff.

It can, however, be argued that, comparing the initial years when the SPR came into being to the present day, the organisation has become at least partially a 'slumbering giant' of paranormal research. Its own website currently talks about that early period as being 'The Heroic Age', during which time there were huge censuses on hauntings (*Phantasms of the Living*, 1886) and hallucinations taking place. As well as this, there was active research which resulted in members Hodgson and Davey discovering and demonstrating the ways in which fake séances could be, and were so often, conducted at this time.

Even into the 1930s, the premises of the SPR were used in the same sort of way (if not scale) as Harry Price's National Laboratory. The SPR, for example, boasted a dedicated 'Séance Room' for investigating mediums. It also did key research into altered states of consciousness, pioneered by member George Tyrrell. The conjectures he made that such altered states would have on improving extrasensory perception and clairvoyance are still a key hypotheses worked on in many lab-based ESP experiments to this day.

Whilst still based in Kensington, central London, today the SPR works out of more modest offices. These consist of a staff office and a meeting room, which doubles up as a lending library for a small part of its very impressive collection of books. It does not have an area for experimentation, but would in any case probably correctly claim that much of this work is now done most effectively either by those who it gives research grants to, or by the small but growing band of universities that now dare to pursue such things. What it does not yet perhaps do enough of, however, is what it would call 'spontaneous case research', which most others, including the popular press, would call 'ghost hunting'. Because of the explosion of locally based groups, it is no longer necessarily the first port of call for individuals who are experiencing the paranormal, or the newspapers they may often ring up as a cry for help. Unlike the Ghost Club however, it has not yet developed a tradition for actively trying to gain access to potential paranormal hotspots. I make the above comments as a member of the Spontaneous Case Committee, so cannot myself be exempt from any criticism.

This is not to say that front line investigation in the SPR is by any means totally a phantom of previous times. There is day-today activity, of which the most interesting at present is the research into tape recordings at haunted locations by Spontaneous Case Committee member Barry Colvin. He has made initial conclusions that 'ghostly knocks', as recorded in apparently haunted houses, have an entirely different resonance to knocks of all types made by normal means. The former gradually increases to a peak of sound, while the latter starts at a peak of sound and slowly descends. This research is still ongoing, but the implications are potentially immense. There have also been some high profile investigations in the not too distant past. The most famous of these was undoubtedly the 1980s Enfield Poltergeist case mentioned earlier. This was investigated by SPR members (the late) Maurice Grosse and Guy Playfair. Guy has recently become active again in the Spontaneous Case Committee and his expertise could be invaluable in the future.

I will digress a little on a further notable exception to the SPR's slight recent absence from the actual 'coalface' of paranormal investigation, as this particular case tells us much about differing styles and attitudes to investigations, which will be of great importance to anyone thinking of carrying one out. The case in question is an investigation of a very successful physical medium group who were active in Scole, Norfolkshire. They were extensively investigated in the late 1990s by the experienced investigators Montague Keen, Arthur Ellison and David Fontana. The size and extent of this research led to a book-length report being produced by the SPR in 1999 entitled 'The Scole Report'.

The investigation and report was to cause much debate both inside and outside the society. This was primarily because, unlike the famous medium investigations of the 1930s, they were conducted not at a place of the SPR's choosing, but in the basement of one of the medium's homes. They also took place without either lighting or night vision equipment which, despite the protestations of the investigators, the mediums insisted the spirits would not feel comfortable with.

Nevertheless, the investigators were on the whole convinced by the vast selection of phenomena that they were witness to in a series of sittings. These included spirit-induced photographs, communications, lights, apports and even touching of the witnesses. The report opened up a healthy debate within the society as to whether favourable conclusions can be reached when working under such imperfect circumstances.

On assessing the report, long-standing society member Tony Cornell pointed out (in the report's appendix) that a fairly large number of key controls were missing. These included that:

- *The mediums were never searched.*

- *As previously mentioned, the séances were held in the dark.*

- *The mediums were not restrained, and allowed to sit next to each other.*

- *Music was played during the séances which could have been used to cover up movement.*

- *Velcro armbands intended to show everybody's position were easily removable.*

- *Most of the equipment used was supplied by the mediums.*

However, David Fontana put up a spirited defense of the investigators' approach. He explained that:

> No one supposes that writers, poets, musicians and others who practice the creative arts could produce their best works if they were told by outsiders the precise conditions under which they must labour. And if we have learnt anything from the century and more of investigations undertaken by this society, *it is that mediumship is much closer to an art than a science* [my italics]. Thus investigators are confronted by a dilemma. Generally they are present in the séance rooms as invited guests rather than as major-domos. Should they then insist upon their protocols, at a cost of blank sittings or even exclusions from the séance rooms, or should they accept the status quo and study what is on offer.
>
> ('The Scole Report', p. 440.)

This is an interesting observation, more so when you realise that the late Maurice Grosse of the Enfield Poltergeist fame was actually excluded by the Scole mediums. They objected to him suggesting a poltergeist explanation for the phenomena, which would have not fitted well with the spiritualist-style afterlife explanation that most mediums adhere to. Indeed, the style of and accessibility to a phenomena sometimes makes full controls impossible, and so long as you are aware of the implications it may have on the results, I can see no harm in continuing such an investigation.

Montague Keen defends the report further by pointing out that it is a pitfall to, 'reject a paranormal explanation unless and until all normal possibilities have been rejected.' ('The Scole Report', p. 426). This was, he thought, an impossibly high standard that the report's critics were using.

Montague Keen may well be correct in this. However, there is also a danger in taking this argument just a little further and actually accepting the validity of phenomena gained under these imperfect circumstances. I would suggest that the correct stance to take is simply to list it in the 'interesting but inconclusive' category into which, sadly, the vast majority of good paranormal cases tend to fit.

Despite his exclusion from the group, Maurice Grosse was very supportive of the investigators and would have perhaps disagreed with my conclusions. He stated in a postscript to the main report that:

> It is imperative that a balanced view is taken of all the reported activity as a whole. If in consequence the consensus of opinion is that it is impossible to explain all the experiences in a logical manner then by definition some of the activity is illogical.
>
> ('The Scole Report', p. 448)

Does this though, for example, mean that if we catch a medium cheating nine times, and then on the tenth occasion we cannot provide an obvious explanation, that we should simply accept it as paranormal? Surely most peoples' first thought would be that perhaps the medium had got cleverer in faking phenomena in the meantime? I very much wish I was still in a position to have this debate with Maurice, as it goes to the core of the different types of mindsets that are found within two groups of (equally dedicated and genuine) investigators. The mindset of an investigator is, as you will see, as important as the equipment he or she uses.

In replying to the critics of the report, Arthur Ellison also makes comment regarding the reasons why the three investigators, including himself, may have been selected by the mediums for the project. He states that:

> I think that the reason may be because we had particular psychological characteristics likely to make us catalysts rather than inhibitors. (The Experimenter Effect is surely sufficiently established to be taken into account.) All three of us knew from experience that paranormal phenomena did sometimes take place...

Here, I think Ellison is on dangerous ground. The Experimenter Effect is indeed an established theory stating that disbelief among those who observe actually inhibits the phenomena itself. By its nature, it is a very difficult theory to disprove. However, it is not a theory I have too much time for either.

It is, after all, not a theory that is found in any other branch of science. Imagine Alexander Fleming, on discovering penicillin, explaining to an initially sceptical scientific community that they would have to believe in the ability of mould to kill off bacteria before the penicillin mould would oblige. Now, it can be successfully argued that discovery of the paranormal is unique as it involves the attempted discovery of what could be an intelligent afterlife. Unlike Fleming's penicillin mould, this afterlife could have all the eccentricities of human beings and, indeed, only want to be discovered by those who already believe, or alternatively not be discovered at all. Whilst this is indeed possible, if it were true it would lead to the conclusion that the paranormal cannot be investigated in the scientific sense, as it will only generally occur to those who already believe. It will be impossible, therefore, to present evidence to those who do not.

Thus, while Ellison's observations on the Experimenter Effect could be true, if it were true it would make paranormal investigation impossible for the majority of researchers who do not necessarily fully believe in the afterlife theory. Therefore, if we are to investigate the paranormal we have to first assume that his observations are not correct. Otherwise we might as well all stick to watching horror films to fire our imagination of the unknown.

The Scole investigation finally shows a good example of research work, which in my opinion is just as important as the investigation itself. A key piece of evidence surrounded the mysterious appearance of what appeared to be a wartime edition of the *Daily Mail*, from 1 April 1944, which was shown to be printed in the long-extinct 'Letterpress' printing style. This appeared most impressive until further investigations by Tony Cornell revealed that wartime newspaper memorabilia had been printed in the 1970s and 1980s using the 'Letterpress' style for authenticity. This had included the edition of 1 April 1944. By contacting suppliers of original historic newspapers, he discovered that the *Daily Mail* at the time had normally been printed with a red letterhead, while these replicas had used a black one. The apport from the séance room has a black letterhead, which was certainly indicative of it being a 1970s replica, and therefore more easily obtainable by non-paranormal means.

I have talked at length about the Scole case as it brings up many of the dilemmas an investigator can be faced with, and some of the solutions for tackling them. We will, of course, discuss these further later on in the book. Whatever the rights and wrongs of the case, it is also an excellent example of how the SPR can, and has the resources to, fully dissect a complex case. The fact that they can do it is a huge plus for the organisation, and a good reason for joining.

However, the SPR does far more than just investigations. It runs perhaps one of the most extensive libraries on the paranormal available to its members. A fraction of this is now based in the London offices, but the rest can be called back from its Cambridge

University home on demand. It also has online access to its own extensive journals dating back to the late nineteenth century. These facilities combine to make for an excellent research resource.

The SPR's day-to-day activities include, like the Ghost Club, a good selection of speakers as well as 'study days' on particular topics and a set-piece annual conference over several days. This has a unique range of speakers, from out-and-out traditional ghost hunters to representatives of the paranormal research groups in universities discussing ongoing research into subjects such as telepathy. In all these events, the SPR in no way excludes newer members; it just perhaps has not learnt the old trick of inviting them for a drink to get to know them. Should you make the effort to get to know the activists in the SPR, however, they are on the whole a fascinating bunch of friendly people.

The SPR, despite by its own high standards having a lower rate of front-line activity than was historically the case, is still the essential backbone of paranormal investigations in this country. It remains a most useful society to join for those who wish to do serious research on the paranormal and ghosts.

ASSAP

The last of what I call the 'big three' nationally-based paranormal organisations is the Association for the Scientific Study of Anomalous Phenomena, or ASSAP. Whilst rather long, the name does perfectly describe what ASSAP aims to achieve. This is to ambitiously (and by no means unsuccessfully) provide a presence in all areas of the unexplained, including UFOs and undiscovered animals (which are not primarily covered by the SPR or the Ghost Club). There are not perhaps many non-wordy names that would perfectly describe this function. It still remains rather difficult to say after a couple of pints in the bar after a day-long investigation.

ASSAP was founded relatively recently, in 1981, partly by some key SPR members who thought the SPR at that time was in need of modernization. This caused one of those splits that are unfortunately far too predominant in the world of paranormal groups.

Much of the impetus for the launch of this new society came from the tireless and dynamic scientist Hugh Pincott, who was until then on the SPR council. Partially through advertising for members (which was unheard of at the time), ASSAP was launched with a very respectable roll of about 300 members. A lot of these were young, enthusiastic and very active. I actually joined it myself early on as a college student and obtained much useful and helpful guidance. The organisation has grown in strength and flourishes today, with Hugh still active.

ASSAP may well have meant to become an association that would organise sufficient activities to keep its enthusiastic members happy. It certainly succeeded in doing this for a while, with long-running projects on such things as hauntings and reincarnations. (The latter taught me to be competent, if now a bit rusty, in hypnotic regression techniques). Starting from scratch, and using simply volunteers, such a level of activity would have been unsustainable in the long run. In time though, ASSAP has found a different but equally important niche; that of being an umbrella organisation to provide support for affiliated groups and suitable qualified members to organise their own activities. It carries out this function effectively. For example, in the early 1990s it became one of the first organisations to develop an equipment library, containing the new range of high-tech equipment (EMF meters and the like) that are thought to have a use in the detection of ghostly phenomena.

ASSAP also invented one of the first credible training courses for investigators, insisting that anyone carrying out an investigation on behalf of ASSAP or one of its affiliated groups had a team member who had first successfully completed this course. The course itself consists of a weekend of training and lectures, combined with having to hand in a suitable piece of research work. One colleague of mine once tried (without success) to claim exemption from this course on the grounds that he was a qualified scientist. The fact that this exemption was not granted was, in my opinion, entirely correct. A qualification in one science does not after all qualify you to investigate what we hope may ultimately become another science. In addition to the training, ASSAP also has members with expertise in various fields who will advise and assist on particular aspects of investigations, such as unusual photographs. Thus, all groups affiliated to ASSAP have some level of consistency in the way they work. There are currently just over twenty local groups affiliated to ASSAP. Whilst these represent a small percentage of the total groups that now exist, they include many which are regarded as doing the best investigative work in the field.

When ASSAP itself runs a set-piece investigation, as it does from time to time, it is often as an extension to its training day. As a training exercise they work excellently, but, in my opinion, as investigations they are not quite so successful. This is not because of a lack of expertise in running them. It is simply because they are very 'open house' events with little limit on numbers. You cannot, in my opinion, run a truly effective investigation with perhaps thirty enthusiastic people split into seven groups. If a member of one group has to go to the bathroom mid-session, you can be sure there will be reports of mysterious footsteps (or mysterious running water?) from others. Whilst this specific example is fictitious, it clearly demonstrates the general point I am making. With a group that size, and even with vigorous note-taking, you can never quite be sure what every person in the group is doing. The other problem with such large investigations is what I would call 'equipment fatigue' (the overuse of equipment making it likely the investigator will not record the information properly). With each investigator bringing their own equipment, the result could be cables running everywhere, multiples of cameras pointing at the 'haunted fireplace' (for example) as if tourists on a visit. There is even the possibility of sensitive equipment picking up the functioning of other sensitive equipment.

As with my comments regarding Ghost Club investigations, I in no way mean to be over-critical about ASSAP's techniques, especially in this case where they are in fact primarily used as training exercises. However, from being the infant organisation of the 1980s, ASSAP has now become a leading player in paranormal investigations. The way they do things must also therefore be the subject of analysis in a book that is primarily about trying to find the right way to investigate.

In addition to the above, the association has a reasonably sized book library – though not on the scale of the SPR. What it does not have is regular speakers' meetings in which the membership can meet up with each other. If you wish this however, some of ASSAP's affiliate organisations do just that. It is by far the cheapest of the three organisations to join, which fits nicely with the original aim of inclusiveness. It also has a good website packed with advice rather than past investigations. In short, should you be new to ghost hunting and want to learn fast and in a structured manner, then ASSAP could well prove ideal.

We can summarise the three organisations I have been describing:

- *The Ghost Club – a social and debating club with some good investigations to participate in.*

- *The SPR – a wealth of academic know-how, a research library to die for, and an excellent and stimulating annual conference.*

- *ASSAP – an umbrella organisation setting high standards in groups and training which also initiates investigations from time to time.*

You will see that none of these organisations are actually in direct competition with each other, as they all have a slightly different function that compliment each other well. It would even appear that they were designed to be interlinked and cover the subject from all angles. Based on the above, you would think it natural the three organisations would work in close co-operation, and share results. Sadly, the nature of societies in general seems to include a fierce independence, and although this is to the detriment of paranormal investigation as a whole, co-operation is often the exception rather than the rule.

I mention this as it is even more relevant should you seek to find a locally-based research group, which by its nature has less resources and members than a nationally-based one. As there could be up to 1,000 such groups around the country, I could not hope to comment on them individually. The one bit of advice I would give is that the group you choose should be in contact with others in the field. If it is not then deep down there is every chance the group already has a set agenda of beliefs, or is just doing investigations for the fun of doing them. It may well not be very good at doing them in any case. If you are looking for a group that will be open-minded and serious in its approach, one that shares its ideas and outlooks is the best place you can start.

Just as an example, I will comment on two local groups that I have found to be particularly impressive through my dealings with them. Both affiliate themselves formally to ASSAP and also work with the SPR. The first of these is Parasearch, which has been running since 1986, long before the boom in local groups started, and covers paranormal activity in the West Midlands. It was set up by David Taylor, who somehow manages to fit in being a graphic designer in-between all the investigations and research carried out. They even have time to organise occasional conferences, which are open to all. To become a member you would normally have to show some level of skill or expertise so perhaps it's not a group for first-timers. Having passed them cases in the past, however, I have always felt they are in very skilled and capable hands. Also of great importance is the fact that Parasearch accepts that a single group cannot have total knowledge of the subject and have formed formal contacts with experts in such areas as physics and photography.

Moving further northwards to the Merseyside area, you find the similarly-named but totally independent Para.Science organisation. This was set up in the mid-1990s by Steve Parsons and Ann Winsper. Steve can be forthright in his views that he believes that Para.Science is the most thorough and professional organisation in the country. It is quite possible that he could be right. Their 750-hour (in total) investigation of phenomena at the Cammel Laird Shipyard would certainly be considered as thorough. In addition, both Steve and Ann have done relevant scientific PHDs, so their understanding of the use (and misuse) of the range of ghost hunting equipment is second to none.

I actually first met them when giving a talk on the use and misuse of equipment at an SPR conference. Here they promptly (and correctly) pointed out that the slide I was using of a colleague using an EMF (electromagnetic field) meter was actually incorrect, as the meter would be far less effective at picking up variations in the electromagnetic field when placed low down on the floor as it was in the photo. Since then, they have become trusted, respected and very thought-provoking colleagues. Their group is exclusive, with membership being by strict invitation, and they do not work with other local groups in the same way that Parasearch do. However, they do, as I mentioned before, work closely with both ASSAP and the SPR. Perhaps most importantly, you do get the feeling that some of their investigations might really discover something of importance.

Paranormal investigation groups of whatever level of evolution or sophistication should not be muddled in any way with what I will finally call 'paranormal tourism groups'. A number of groups have been set up in the last decade or so which rent out high profile haunted premises for an evening and, for a fee, will let members of the public participate in a ghost hunt. The aim of these groups in many cases is to make a profit for their efforts. Many researchers hate this type of organisation, though personally I think they do little harm if properly run. There are many people who may not want to actually spend days and weeks (or as with Para.Science, 750 hours) in the search for truth. If all someone wants is the experience of spending the night in a 'haunted house', who are we to be snobbish about it? Should that be all you are after, just take care to ensure – as with all things – that the organisers are established and professional. Having never been an active sampler of 'ghost tourism', I cannot make recommendations for the best organisers of such things. A good search on the internet will certainly give you a varied choice.

This chapter has explored the options for an individual who wishes to start serious ghost hunting. As you can see, the options are now many and varied – far more varied than even a decade before. There has been one further important change that does not really fit into this chapter. This is the tentative start of serious research in some of our universities. Whilst this is irrelevant on one level to the budding ghost hunter (unless he or she is doing a degree in such a place), on another level it is vital. Universities and other academic institutions have the potential to change the whole nature of paranormal investigations. For that reason alone, they deserves a short chapter to themselves so as to explain further.

three

THE STATE OF ACADEMIC PARAPSYCHOLOGY TODAY

Universities don't hunt ghosts

This chapter was originally planned to be the final section of the previous one. Such though is the difference in approach between universities and private groups, it would not have fitted comfortably in a chapter that mentioned the words 'ghost hunting'. Since the time Harry Price had to turn down his placement at Bonn University, there has long been a hope that paranormal investigation could be put on a more proper academic footing. Recently this has in fact started to happen, although not as yet quite in the way most investigators would have envisaged.

Prior to 1985, there was not a department in any UK university that specialised in parapsychology, let alone one with members willing to get their hands dirty investigating spontaneous paranormal incidents. There were one or two lecturers, such as the pioneering John Beloff, who taught the subject since 1962 at Edinburgh University. However, this was only as part of the Department of Psychology.

However, when the famous writer Arthur Keostler died in a suicide pact with his wife in 1983, it was revealed in his will that he would bequest his entire estate to establish a Chair of Parapsychology at a British university. Keostler had always had a keen interest in the paranormal, and like many others had obviously wished its investigation to cease being an eccentricity and become more of a mainstream academic subject.

Although at the time John Beloff was on the point of retirement, his experience in teaching successfully at Edinburgh over the previous twenty years, combined with Edinburgh's actual enthusiasm (unlike some other universities) for such a position, made Edinburgh the prime and ultimately successful candidate.

Again with the help of Beloff, a successful candidate was found for the position. This was the American Robert Morris. Morris had already worked in parapsychology as a lecturer at the University of California, and was widely respected in the field. Morris helped set up what became know as the Koestler Parapsychology Unit (KPU) and at the time of his unfortunate and premature death in 2004, aged sixty-two, 100 undergraduates had included the subject in their course. In addition, thirty postgraduates had taken things much further, often to the point of wanting to teach the subject themselves. So as the existence of the KPU gradually made parapsychology more respectable and a few other universities very gradually introduced it, there have been British-trained academics available to take up the mantle. The KPU today has three members of staff and is innovatively introducing an online course in the subject which will greatly increase its accessibility.

Significant departments now exist at a small but growing number of universities, including the University of Northampton's Centre for the Study of Anomalous Psychological Processes. This is a department of six people led by a former lecturer at the KPU, Deborah Delaney, and includes at least two former KPU students, Simon Sherwood and Chris Roe. Deborah is also currently President of the SPR. Northampton lays claims on its website to being one of only four places in the world which is actively pursuing research in, 'The experience and phenomena of extrasensory perception (ESP) and psychokinesis (PK), and experiences of unusual and/or exceptional quality, such as mystical and peak experiences'.

In layman's terms, this is actual frontline research into the existence (or otherwise) of paranormal phenomena. When you add to that the good links they keep with researchers outside of the universities, the Northampton department is surely a resource of huge potential.

The small department run by Richard Wiseman at the University of Hertfordshire has a rather different approach. Initially a conjurer and one of the youngest members of the Magic Circle, Wiseman also studied as a postgraduate at the KPU. He has also had a great deal of success publicising his activities in the media. The combination of a unique insight into the potential for any faking through his conjuring experience, combined with his understanding of how the mind can be tricked, makes him well-equipped to seek out normal explanations to apparently paranormal events.

Wiseman's success with the media has been to his department's advantage as he has shown an inclination to experiment outside the walls of his university. He has conducted investigations at such high profile sites as Hampton Court, where the phenomena may actually be happening, rather than simply staying within the confines of his academic base. Encouraging universities to participate outside of their comfort zone is perhaps one of the key elements in improving investigations. In so much as Wiseman has helped make this a respectable thing to do, he has surely made an important contribution.

A more recent addition to the university-based groups comes from the very haunted city of York, although it is probably only a coincidence that in 2006, York University set up their Anomalous Experience Research Unit (AERU). This is not a parapsychology department in itself, however, or a branch of the university's psychology department, but an interdisciplinary unit attached, perhaps uniquely, to the sociology department.

Perhaps because of this, the official approach to the subject is rather different. The aims of the unit as per their website are to research the:

❧ *Language of anomalous experiences.*

❧ *Exploration and application of new social scientific methods for the study of anomalous experiences.*

❧ *Role of the researcher in the study of anomalous experiences; ethics and reflexivity.*

❧ *Social and cultural context of parapsychology and its relationship to the social sciences.*

Unlike its counterparts at Herefordshire or Northampton, the AERU does not specifically mention establishing whether any of the phenomena actually exists. This may or may not be an indication that such departments still need to tread carefully to be taken seriously in a university environment. However, since its founding, this still relatively young department has done some key research into such areas as mediums and altered states of consciousness.

The Anomalistic Psychology Research Group (APRG) of Goldsmiths, University London does tackle the subject in a more direct, experimental way. It attempts to discover whether the causes of strange occurrences are paranormal or whether there is another, possibly psychologically-based explanation.

What makes this group a little different, however, is the approach by its departmental head, Professor Christopher French. His views on the paranormal appear to be sceptical. Slight clues in this direction could indeed be the fact that he helps edit *The Skeptics* magazine and currently advertises the popular 'Skeptics In The Pub' debating group on his department's university web page.

Some in paranormal investigation associate sceptics with unbelievers and debunkers and do not like working with them. It is perhaps fair to say that the mediums in the Scole group who found Maurice Grosse's poltergeist theories unpalatable may well have taken more objection to some of Chris French's theories. Sceptics, however, are not necessarily out-and-out disbelievers, and are possibly best summed up by a quote from the APRG's web page:

Anomalistic psychology may be defined as the study of extraordi-
nary phenomena of behaviour and experience, including (but not
restricted to) those which are often labelled 'paranormal'. It is directed
towards understanding bizarre experiences that many people have
without assuming a priori that there is anything paranormal involved.
It entails attempting to explain paranormal and related beliefs and
ostensibly paranormal experiences in terms of known psychological
and physical factors.

The important part here is that the group is 'attempting to explain'
the paranormal in terms of the known psychological and physical. They hold open the possibility that if their attempts to do so
fail, they will be left with evidence which will, at the least, indicate that the paranormal may exist. What perhaps actually irritates
some out-and-out believers (who could also be accused of being
sceptical towards normal explanations), is that having seen Chris
French speak on several occasions and met him once or twice, it is
clear to me he is actually rather successful in fulfilling his department's aims. He does not rubbish anything, but provides some
very compelling arguments for a normal explanation of many
types of phenomena. This can seem perhaps bland and dull to us
adventurers trying to find a new type of truth or reality. However,
any such truth or reality has to first be checked to see if it is 'true'
and 'real'. In my opinion, any experiment or investigation should
include a 'Chris French' type of sceptic on them to give a balanced viewpoint.

The fact that the Goldsmiths unit works in an open-minded
way can further be shown by the ongoing research it is currently
doing with the biologist Dr Rupert Sheldrake. Sheldrake's theories of morphic resonance (a living, developing universe with
its own inherent memory) put him firmly in the field of those
who postulate explanations beyond current science. For a time,
these theories also made him a controversial figure amongst
more conventional scientists. French and Sheldrake, however,
are currently trying to jointly replicate some successful research
that Sheldrake previously carried out on telephone telepathy

(the ability to predict when someone is about to call you on the telephone). This experiment strikes me as an ideal way forward. When two people of integrity, intelligence and slightly different outlooks on a subject work together, any agreed results will surely be all the more valuable when presented as evidence for or against the paranormal.

As mentioned in the previous chapter, one of the most successful paranormal investigation groups, Para.Science, is based in the Liverpool area. It is also home to both of the final two university departments I will mention. The Consciousness Transpersonal Psychology Unit at Liverpool John Moores University does important research into both the nature of consciousness and the psychology of spiritual development.

This is nicely complimented by the Parapsychology Research Group within the Department of Psychology, Liverpool Hope University, which directly studies potential anomalous or psychic experiences.

There is therefore a growing, if still fledgling, presence in the academic community investigating the realms of the unknown. Many of these academics are members of the Parapsychological Association, a worldwide group first established in 1957 with approximately 300 members, which acts as a useful umbrella organisation for such work. Perhaps more importantly from the point of view of future co-operation with non-academic paranormal researchers, several are active in the SPR. As well as Deborah Delaney, who leads the Northampton University unit, being SPR President, Chris Roe also of the Northampton Unit is editor of its journal and proceedings, and Paul Stevens, formerly a researcher with the Koestler unit in Edinburgh University, is also on the SPR council.

The SPR is thus a body which at least gives the possibility for scientists to work with other like-minded investigators on a common purpose. Unfortunately the actual level of this type of joint work is currently very low. I may have amusingly subtitled this chapter 'Universities don't hunt ghosts' as a contrast to the previous chapter on the state of ghost hunting today. This is, however, very much a true statement. In fact, you would struggle to see even a mention of the word 'ghost' on the websites of most of these units.

During most SPR conferences that I have attended, there has always been light-hearted, but perhaps very insightful, commentary that it is really two conferences rolled into one. Often you could tell what category of speaker was talking by seeing which part of the audience had gone out for a breath of fresh air. These two parts of the conference were no less than the laboratory-based parapsychologists that this chapter has been discussing and the site-based paranormal investigators discussed in the previous chapter. Both groups will happily eat together, drink together, talk together, joke together but (with some exceptions) rarely work together in their search to explain the unexplained.

Why though has the development of these two so closely related disciplines been separate? More importantly, is the present state of things the norm, or are there practical ways in which we can start to make changes?

Personally, I have reached no definite conclusions as to whether such separate development of the two fields is avoidable, but there must be a very practical desire that it is not so. Many paranormal investigations undoubtedly need the technique and scientific rigour that experienced parapsychologists could add. In a field of study, however, where the main theories state that phenomena may only occur under specific empirical and geographic conditions, it is still often due to the pioneering spirit of paranormal investigators that these specific locations are investigated in the first place. It therefore seems sane, sensible and indeed scientific that the two disciplines should complement each other, rather than working apart in parallel.

Having noticed this division, I recently explored it further by conducting a questionnaire on what people regarded as good investigative techniques, to which I received a number of interesting replies. Two responses, both from very experienced researchers, could perhaps be examples of the differing approaches that may be commonly found in each of the disciplines. Commenting on a section about using scientifically unproven equipment and methods such as psychics, dowsing rods, planchettes, etc., one respondent argued along the lines that, 'All scientifically unproven techniques should be excluded from investigations because they are all open to fraud (either consciously or unconsciously), and should therefore not be submitted as (scientific) evidence.' However, the second respondent countered this with the argument that, 'As there are no portable instruments that are capable of measuring energy fluctuations at quantum physics levels, we need at least for now to rely on mediums who do appear to have some access to systems that are influenced by quantity energy variations.'

Both these answers are very coherent, but perhaps in a general way sum up the careful and cautious approach found more often in parapsychology against the more swashbuckling and far-reaching theorising of many paranormal researchers. Neither is wrong, but both are very different.

I would possibly take this undoubted generalisation further in claiming that there is perhaps one major flaw in their approach that each community has a tendency to suffer from, and which may make the other wary of co-operation. In the case of quite a wide sector of paranormal investigators, it is a failure to implement research and conclusions with what is known as 'Occam's razor'. This is a kind of *modus operandi* clarified by William of Occam as far back as the fourteenth century which can be summarised as, 'all things being equal the simplest solution is the best one'. There is sometimes a tendency for at least a significant proportion of paranormal investigators to forget this. I have not talked to Chris French specifically on this subject, but his general comments tend to indicate he follows this ancient piece of advice.

After the apparent exposure of a medium in a national paper in the 1980s, where witnesses were confronted with initially impressive phenomena (until the magically appearing spirit flowers were eventually detected hidden within the medium's tape recorder), I was fascinated by some of the theories that were still used to counter the fraud hypothesis. An experienced and very capable paranormal researcher who had worked with this particular medium spoke to me of conclusions which I would summarise as follows; that as the paranormal was the 'normal' to the medium, he could quite happily produce apports from a variety of sources without it seeming to him he was cheating. Another counter-fraud theory used in this and similar cases has stated that while the pressure of being investigated could cause a medium to cheat, early phenomena of the same type was probably genuine as the medium wasn't caught cheating then. If you remember our previous discussion on the Scole case, this is similar to the logical conclusion I surmised would follow from Maurice Grosse's comments. Now while both these statements are not strictly speaking illogical, they do fly in the face of Occam's razor and normal scientific theorising. Thus, this belief pattern could well create a division between the two subjects.

However, there is also perhaps a trend within the scientific community to forget the fact that science rarely, if ever, achieves absolute truth and has arguably evolved in a series of what the philosopher Khun called 'scientific paradigms'. These are models of the world that are discarded as their usefulness at predicting the outcome of experimentation diminishes. Medieval theories (thought to be quite self-evidently true at the time) of the Earth being flat were in due course replaced by Newtonian physics, which whilst itself undoubtedly based on good scientific experimentation, has long been superseded by the theories of Einstein. Each of these theories was supported in their time by scientists, yet none of them, including our current theories, are likely to be wholly accurate.

Where this is important to the paranormal is that, by definition, discovering proof of most paranormal hypotheses would involve a whole new scientific paradigm – a whole new set of rules with which to work. To discover such proofs, it is therefore arguably both acceptable and necessary to experiment using techniques and apparatus whose theories are not yet accepted within science, provided, of course, that the principles of the experimentation are scientifically sound. Yet scientists throughout history have had a habit of holding to their current beliefs, sometimes with a near evangelical certainty. This can seem frustrating and stifling to those who wish to explore beyond current scientific boundaries. As one of the responses to my questionnaire further pointed out, 'When physical items disappear before your eyes and heavy objects rise in the air and shoot across the room, it is clear our scientific principles cannot explain the paranormal. Investigative techniques must therefore be used which science has not yet accepted.'

A respected and very experienced paranormal investigator surprised me by commenting at a conference recently that the reason he could not work with parapsychologists was that he found them 'boring'. Perhaps what he was really trying to explain was his frustration that some parapsychologists only try to prove what would be a 'new science' of the paranormal using the methods acceptable to current science. (Alternatively, he may just have found them plain boring, but I hope that was not the case as it rather ruins my argument.)

What I have said may be part of the reason why there is wariness from the two disciplines to work more closely together. Can this be overcome, and can people with useful skills but different approaches work together on the same project?

In my view, assuming that there are no personality clashes or excessive dogmatism, to have both types of people or teams involved in a project would in fact be little short of a 'dream ticket' for the perfect investigation. Imagine the insight you could get from comparing both sets of conclusions, which combined would make for an excellent and rounded report – the rigour of parapsychology's scientific technique combined with the more accessible style of the paranormal researcher.

Should both parties come to the same conclusions, be it in support of the apparent paranormal hypothesis or otherwise, this would provide any subsequent report with a much larger level of overall credibility. Thus you see my level of enthusiasm at the joint experimentation that I mentioned between Chris French and Rupert Sheldrake, who although both qualified scientists, can still be put into the contrasting camps of 'rational sceptic' and 'rational believer'.

What, however, could be the reasons for the delay in full co-operation between ghost hunters (the words I have not yet used in this chapter) and the academic parapsychologists? I will conclude this chapter by trying to answer this, and make suggestions for overcoming barriers.

In the present academic climate it is clearly possible to study parapsychology or something similar. However, it still may be a problem 'politically' for universities to be seen to be promoting ghost hunting-type field research so soon after laboratory-based research has been taken under their wing. I mentioned that some of the university-based units such as York seem to mainly research around the psychological and sociological implications of the phenomena rather than to actually test its reality. Is this simply what they feel their own discipline should entail, or is there an element of peer pressure to ensure credibility within the wider confines of a university, or even a need to follow projects for which research grants are available?

If parapsychologists were to involve themselves more in field-work, are they in a position to obtain additional expertise from other departments of their faculty? For example, could they get acoustic or electromagnetic expertise from Electronics or Physics departments? Alternatively, would other departments shy away from such involvement in these areas at this point in time? It is worth noting that whilst there have been many students of para-psychology, there have been only a handful of paraphysics students. It seems then that there may well still be paranormal no-go areas for many university departments that could otherwise be of great assistance.

Even if we assume that support is available, what type of support, if any, would paranormal investigators like from para-psychologists? I have given a strong preference towards greater co-operation. Is this preference shared by most paranormal researchers? I have already mentioned that Barry Colvin, a col-league of mine on the SPR's Spontaneous Case Committee, was recently looking for acoustic experts to validate some research on the unusual resonance of ghostly knocks. Think of the progress that could be made if parapsychology departments could provide guidance on such projects and could in turn use the resources of other departments within a university.

Could paranormal investigators assist parapsychologists, perhaps by doing a first filter of potential field investigations? Parapsychologists may be more interested in joining in research in more credible cases. An initial look at cases by paranormal investigators would help the scientific community avoid being sucked into any into any pitfalls of the 'talking mongoose' type (one of the more surreal investigations by Harry Price that I made mention of earlier).

Even when unable to directly assist in paranormal investigations at haunted locations, is there any back up assistance parapsychologists can, and would wish, to provide? This could be especially important with people-centred phenomena discovered by paranormal investigators which are, in principle, quite verifiable under laboratory conditions.

Perhaps, though, the fundamental question is: does each of the related disciplines really respect what the other is trying to do? Are the occasional catcalls and criticisms between the two branches of investigation just good-humoured banter or something that goes very much deeper?

I do not as yet have the answer to these questions, but if you are reading this book as an amateur paranormal field researcher, ask yourself if you make all the effort that you should to get more impressive results further scrutinised? If you read this book as a parapsychologist, ask yourself if there is not worth in using your skills outside of your laboratory more often? If you come from neither of these categories, and read this book as a normal (hopefully), avid reader, then please read on with an open mind.

four

So What Are Ghosts Anyway?

You cannot hunt what you do not know

So far we have raced through over 2,000 years of ghost hunting history and explored the current ghost hunting 'scene' (for want of a better expression) as it stands today. I have thrown in some terms perhaps a trifle interchangeably – such as 'ghost', 'spirit' and 'poltergeist' – of which I hope most readers (be they ghost hunters or not) will have at least a general understanding. I have done this so as to avoid starting a book on an interesting subject with a chapter on definitions. If we are to talk about ghost hunting techniques with any precision, however, such a chapter eventually has to be written, and the time has thus come to bite the bullet. In any case, we must define what we are hunting before we start to hunt it.

The Spirit Theory of Ghosts

For much of the nineteenth and twentieth centuries, the quest was straightforward. Spiritualism had, after all, rejuvenated investigation into ghosts and it therefore seemed natural to start with the hypothesis that we were investigating the existence or otherwise of the spirit of a dead person remaining on earth, perhaps in a place to which he or she had affinity. In the case of séances, such spirits would be seen as already having moved to a better place, but just paying a flying visit back to *terra firma* to communicate with a loved one. Let us call this theory the 'spirit' theory of ghosts.

While this is always instinctively what we think of as being a ghost, there is actually surprisingly little activity in haunted houses that fit this theory to the exclusion of all others. It is rare, if ever, that ghosts strike up a conversation. They seem to have vocal chords in that they may sigh, moan or even occasionally scream. Rarely, however, do they seem to communicate directly to a normal person.

Communication, when it does come, normally occurs via a third party. This may be a medium, or it could be through a Ouija board or planchette. We will say more of these devices later, but suffice to say for now that these are devices through which it may be possible for more than one person to communicate with a 'spirit', should one actually exist.

The problem here is that if evidence for spirit intelligence generally only comes through third parties, is not the conversation struck or the information obtained far more likely to actually come from the third party (perhaps subconsciously) than from the 'spirit'? We mentioned Occam's razor in the last chapter. Now, surely one of the most basic applications of this would be to assume that information comes from the known consciousness that is delivering it, rather than some kind of invading spirit consciousness.

However, the important part of Occam's razor is that it applies when 'all things remain equal'. There are, of course, instances where a Ouija board or medium may pick up information which is not obviously discoverable by the receiver(s). In such cases, however, theories of ESP (mind reading) may be equally applicable. To get definite evidence of an afterlife through a receiving third party, the information would not only have to be shown to be unknown to them, but also highly unlikely to be known by anyone who is in any way connected with the investigation. There is then another hurdle to climb. For that obscure bit of information to be evidential, it must first be shown to be correct, which by the fact that it must be obscure is often no mean feat. The sort of communication you want to pick up, for example, would be directions to a box in a secret panel that contain papers with some long-forgotten information about the communicating spirit. Such a communication would exclude virtually all other theories other than the spirit one. That would also be a ghost hunter's birthday, Christmas and national lottery win combined, for sadly it just doesn't happen like that very often.

In an investigation that I organised in the underground remains of the Clerkenwell House of Detention prison museum (now sadly closed down), psychics came up with a strong communication by an entity identifying itself as 'John Shaw'. This may or may not have been a genuine communication from a discarnate spirit. The point, however, was that the House of Detention was a remand and debtors' prison, with a populace of 10,000 unfortunates a year at its peak. Even with the most sophisticated piece of research, the facts of the matter were never going to be established.

Of more use from an evidential point of view was another private investigation in a London council house. Here, the mediums we worked with managed to correctly identify the sex and prime location of the apparent ghost. In such cases, however, even assuming there is no 'natural' explanation, an ESP explanation between the psychics and the owners of the house can be seen as equally likely.

If only we could all be as fortunate as Harry Price who, in his famous investigations into Borley Rectory, apparently all but managed that 'birthday, Christmas, national lottery' moment. This happened during séances run in Streatham (many miles from Borley) by others involved in the investigation. The participants in these séances picked up information regarding the placing of the bones of a murdered nun, 'Mary Lairre', under the cellar floor. Subsequently, a female jawbone was in fact discovered. Despite the controversy surrounding Harry Price and the possibility that such an artefact may have been added there after the séance, such events do show that the 'spirit' theory of ghosts should in no way be totally discarded. We shall simply put it a little onto the back burner whilst other possibilities are explored.

The Stone Tape or Residual Haunting Theory.

This theory actually got its popular name from a 1972 classic ghost story shown on the BBC, not surprisingly called *The Stone Tape*. The claim here is that ghosts are in fact an audio or visual recording of certain types of happenings, possibly of strong emotional content, such as unexpected deaths or murders. As such, the ghost would not pose any intelligence; it would merely be a projection of happenings from previous times.

When you think about it there is certainly much circumstantial evidence to make this theory attractive. After all, by their nature ghosts seem to be rather repetitive creatures. Returning to Borley Rectory again, the Borley Nun when not (possibly) trying to communicate with the residents of Streatham via séances had, like most other ghosts, very basic movements up and down the garden, so much so that this route became known as the Nun's Walk. Long after Harry Price had died, the nun continued to be seen in the same vicinity, being observed for no less than twelve minutes in the early 1970s by a team of ghost hunters lead by a Mr Croome-Hollingsworth. In all that time the nun apparently gave no signs of communication, finally disappearing into a pile of building bricks.

Perhaps even better evidence for this theory is demonstrated in the famous incident which took place in York. From the 1920s through to the late 1950s there were sightings in the Treasurer's House of ghostly Roman Legionnaires. The best-publicised and most authenticated sighting was made in 1953 by a workman named Harry Martindale, who saw about twenty soldiers walk out of the cellar wall before eventually disappearing again. The story was authenticated by the fact that Martindale, only eighteen at the time, described the soldiers as carrying round shields, which is not the typical Roman Legionnaires attire of large, rectangular shields that you would see in films. However, it is known to historians that auxiliary troops did carry such shields, something that a 1950s teenager was hardly likely to be aware of. Why though would a group of long-dead Roman soldiers decide to walk through a cellar? Now here is where the 'stone tape' theory really comes into its own. Martindale did not actually see the soldier's entire bodies, as part of their legs seemed obscured by the cellar floor. Later excavations were to find a Roman road about 18ins under the base of the cellar. Now an intelligent ghost would surely realise there is little point walking a long-buried track and would have interacted with Martindale in some way, which they did not. A projection, however, would have had no such choice in the matter, projecting themselves in the very spot as they marched tensely to an uncertain fate nearly two millennia ago.

If you remember, I talked previously about the writer Thiselton-Dyer who, at the turn of the twentieth century, speculated why castles and old homes seem to be more haunted than modern flats. Being a man of religion, he came up with the plausible 'spirit-led' theory that it may be because an old house's history made it more likely that people had died in sudden and untoward circumstances and had not received religious rites. However, the 'stone tape' theory comes up with what is at least an equally plausible notion that it might be the very essence of the materials used in building (old, thick, porous stones as opposed, for example, to modern, thin, pre-fabricated concrete) that acts as a better conductor for the recording.

The above gives good circumstantial evidence for the 'stone tape' or residual ghost theory. However, 'stone tape' is perhaps not a strictly accurate description, as there has been much speculation that materials other than stones or building fabrics can hold the essence of past events. In fact, there has even been an effort to get such a notion into the scientific mainstream.

Tom Lethbridge, a famous writer on dowsing during the 1960s, had also noticed the propensity of ghostly-type phenomena to appear either close to water or in a climate of damp. He had already done much work showing what appeared to be the powerful magnetic-type field that water seems to generate and which can be picked up by sensitive or trained people via a dowsing rod. From there, it was only one step further to hypothesise that the fields generated by either streams or a damp environment could in some way produce the right trigger for projecting an image from the past. His book *Ghost and Divining Rod*, published in 1963, fully explained this tantalising theory. If true, this could also explain why damp, old, historic buildings could more frequently be the sites of hauntings. Taken to its logical conclusion, ghosts would then be sent on their way not by an exorcism, but by the installation of dehumidifiers and central heating.

Lethbridge gleaned this theory from his personal experience and other anecdotal evidence, so whilst well-researched it is still in its way basically circumstantial. Lethbridge died in 1971, but over a decade later, in 1984, some mainstream (if controversial) scientific research was to tie in well with his theories.

Dr Jacques Benveniste, former research director at the French National Institute for Medical Research, and an expert in allergies, discovered an unexpected side effect in his experiments into allergy systems in 1984. His experiments involved diluting a substance in water to a degree where the diluted substance was no longer there and only the water molecules remained. However, in experiments he found that reactions took place as if the original non-water molecules were still there. It was as if water molecules themselves had a memory of what they had previously come into contact with; in many ways, basically the same concept suggested by Lethbridge. While not fully accepted by all scientists, the research of Benveniste has never been disproved. It remains one of those anomalies outside of current scientific understanding which, in the past, have often mounted up to show that a new scientific theory or paradigm is needed. Could such a new future science allow the possibility of residual ('stone tape') ghosts? Only time will tell!

Poltergeists

The word 'poltergeist' is literally translated from the German, meaning 'a noisy ghost'. It is actually used by investigators to cover the variety of phenomena which appear to interact directly with the non-supernatural environment, and often the people in that environment. Poltergeist phenomena can include objects being thrown across the room, bangs and taps on walls and tables by unseen forces (sometimes with an intelligible message), and disruption of electrical equipment. In some extreme cases, scratches and minor injuries to the residents of an infested site can also be involved. Let me emphasise at this point, however, that not only are such injuries rare, when they do occur they are inevitably superficial. Descriptions by people who have been hit by flying objects have even described how they appear to slow down at the last moment, as if controlled by something or someone.

It seems that in some ways the poltergeist category of ghosts have extracted all the 'sexy' bits from the other categories. If, however, they are all just different facets of the same entity, why do we use the separate term of 'poltergeist'? If a ghost is being noisy, is it not still a ghost? If this is so, then why the new name? Such a claim is indeed what many who follow the 'spirit' theory of ghosts would make. That poltergeist activities are the parts of the phenomena which show that a ghost has intelligence, and if it shows intelligence surely this must be from a spirit remaining on earth? They would further argue that it is impossible for a thing without intelligence to tap out a message and 'throw' an object.

There is, of course, a great deal of validity in this argument. Indeed, such phenomena must surely be caused by an intelligent entity. Must it, however, be an intelligent 'dead' entity?

Those who do not support the 'spirit' theory of ghosts would tend to argue that poltergeist phenomena are an entirely different kind of phenomena compared to apparitions which may be explained by such theories as the 'stone tape'. They would refer to fairly strong evidence that poltergeists often seem to be people-centred phenomena, which occur primarily when the key person who appears to trigger the phenomena is present. Such people are primarily adolescents who may, in their rapid state of growth and change, have the capacity under certain, possibly stressful, situations to engage in spontaneous psychokinesis (PK); the ability to move objects purely through the power of the mind. It is further argued that such PK can be the result of the adolescent's subconscious mind or even by an alter ego or split personality. The adolescent would thus be an innocent victim as well as the cause.

Looking back at the Enfield Poltergeist case, there were certainly many facets which could be explained by the spontaneous PK theory. Janet Hodgson, who appeared to be the main catalyst for the phenomena, was only eleven, whilst her sister was just a few years older. Whilst the two main investigators, Grosse and Playfair, found the type of phenomena quickly precluded a fraud theory, it was certainly true that the phenomena centred on the children and only rarely occurred when they were not there. Slightly more confusing was the taking over of Janet's vocal chords by an entity called Bill, who claimed to have died in the house. This could offer valid support to the 'spirit' theory of ghosts, whose supporters would claim that Janet acted as an involuntary medium and was in effect 'possessed'. An equally valid explanation, however, would be a case of split personality.

So can we come to any tentative conclusions as to whether poltergeist phenomena is spontaneous PK, or whether it is simply a 'spirit' indulging in noisy activities to gain attention?

Alan Gauld and A.D. Cornell published the book *Poltergeists* in 1979 (Routledge and Kegan Paul) to survey previous cases and did in fact come to some conclusions on this matter. Taking over 500 historical cases and then discarding nearly 200 as possible frauds, they concluded that whilst the majority of the non-fraud cases may have indicated subconscious PK or a living agent, there were also some cases that indicated the work of an intelligent supernatural entity. This would make the possibility of their being two causes of poltergeist phenomena a feasible theory. Personally, I think it is unlikely that one style of phenomena might have two separate causes and it would be better perhaps at this stage to simply say that we are not sure what causes a poltergeist.

David Fontana, always a stout and rational defendant of the afterlife theory, pointed out in the *Journal of the Society for Psychical Research* (Vol. 68.4, No. 877, p. 200) that in his:

... two-year investigation of the 'responsive poltergeist' case in Cardiff (Fontana, 1991,1992), the evidence, much of it witnessed by myself, strongly supported the presence of a discarnate intelligence. If the phenomena were the result of PK from the living, we would have to suppose previously undiscovered macro-PK abilities in three of the four adults in the family group involved (there were no children or adolescents), since phenomena occurred in the sole presence of each of these three. We would also have to suppose that I had such abilities, since phenomena took place when I was alone in the building and the family were some 300 miles away.

Put like that, it is clear that we cannot, despite its undoubted appeal, simply accept the spontaneous PK notion of poltergeists, and there is very much more work to be done both in proving their existence to the outside world and in defining what they are. In some ways this is no bad thing. Most people would like ghosts to be some kind of indication of the afterlife, and it would perhaps be a little sad if that theory ever gets to the stage where the evidence meant it was discarded. Still, if it did, proving PK would not be a bad consolation.

The above are perhaps the three main types, or theories, of ghosts that most ghost hunters will come across in their lifetimes. There are, however, a number of further types of ghostly phenomena that do not fit comfortably into any of these categories.

Crisis Apparitions

These seem to be a special sort of apparition that occur at the point of death or near death, normally of a loved one. They tantalisingly could be seen as the spirit's last visit to a loved one, or a dying mind sending out its last messages by a kind of super-ESP.

While not common, there are a good series of well-attested examples throughout the history of the paranormal. Perhaps one of the best accounts was the death of Vice-Admiral George Tyron in 1893 when his ship, HMS *Victoria*, was accidentally rammed by another British ship, HMS *Camperdown*. Due to Tyron's pigheaded sense of duty, he attempted to beach his vessel to save her and thus lost the chance to abandon ship. This action led to the loss of him and over 350 crew members.

At about the same time as the ship was sinking, his wife, Lady Tyron, was hosting a party. To the surprise of all present, Tyron, in full dress uniform, suddenly came in and walked through the room, eventually vanishing through a door. This was as well-witnessed a crisis apparition as you are ever likely to get.

Doppelgangers

Like 'poltergeist', this is a word borrowed from German which, literally translated, means 'double walker'. A doppelganger in the realms of the paranormal though normally means a ghost of oneself which is often seen as an indication of death in the near future. As such, it is not an entity that is to be encouraged, even by the most enthusiastic of ghost hunters. While very rare, there have been a number of famous sightings especially, strangely enough, by writers and poets. Shelley, for example, reported seeing his doppelganger pointing out to sea shortly before his death in a sailing accident, while the French novelist Guy De Muapassant reported frequent sightings of his double self towards the end of his life. One of the most famous sightings was by the German poet Johann Wolfgang von Goethe, who saw his own doppelganger travelling in the opposite direction on a journey, complete with different attire. However, this was not an indication of his death but perhaps some kind of glimpse in the future, for eight years later and travelling in the opposite direction, he suddenly realised that he was wearing exactly the same clothes he had seen worn by his ghostly double.

Animal Ghosts

These come in two distinct varieties. Ghosts of actual dead animals are not in themselves particularly uncommon. An entire book was written about these phenomena in 1913 by the prolific and colourful ghost hunter Elliott O'Donnell. There are many examples to this day of claims of mainly domestic pets visiting after their demise.

Who can tell whether this is wishful thinking on the part of animal lovers? If we take the phenomena at face value however, we find that it sits uncomfortably with all the major paranormal theories. Why would a run-of-the-mill average cat impress itself to such a great extent on the environment when most versions of the 'stone tape' theory of ghosts seem to rely on an event of some emotional intensity triggering the recording? If, as an alternative, we are to accept the 'survivalist' view of ghosts, we enter a theological, spiritualist debate as to whether and which animals have a soul. Nevertheless, such appearances are quite common to this day. The paranormal writer Natalie Osborne-Thomason mentions two examples of dogs returning after death in her book *Walking Through Walls*. One of these examples is particularly interesting, involving a dog called Zebedee who actually appeared in the new house of his owner. Taken at face value, this animal ghost was showing the presence of mind to follow his owner, as he did in life. Such behaviour seems, of course, to much better fit the 'survival theory' than the residual haunting alternative.

The other type of animal apparition is very different, dating back deep into Celtic folklore and is unlikely to have been an animal that actually lived. This is the not infrequent sightings of 'hell hounds' or 'black dogs' which, like doppelgangers, are often interpreted as symbols of impending doom. These are thought to be other supernatural or demonic entities manifesting as an animal, rather than an animal itself. Where folklore ends and fact begins on such matters, no one is sure. The famous 'sighting' of a black dog in the church of Bungay, Suffolk, as long ago as 1577 is still 'celebrated' by a host of place names in the area and a 'black dog' weather vane. Such ancient phenomena in long-gone times of superstition are surely not to be taken literally? However, Janet and Colin Board observe in their book *Alien Animals* that there have been credible sightings of the phenomena around the country right up to the 1970s. The respected University of Northampton parapsychologist Simon Sherwood also claims to have seen one. Just because such things do not fit into our neat little theories of the paranormal, it does not mean that they can be lightly discounted.

Even more the stuff of legends, you will find a number of what I will call 'fringe categories' of apparitions such as fairies, elementals and mermaids. I mention these in a ghost hunting book simply because you will inevitably come across reports of such things from time to time and will need to decide whether they are simply delusion, a misinterpretation of a different type of paranormal event, or phenomena in their own right. It is worth remembering that in the early part of the twentieth century, fairy phenomena were taken seriously by respected people such as the author of the Sherlock Holmes series, Sir Arthur Conan Doyle. In 1920, Conan Doyle was perhaps rather foolishly taken in by the almost certainly fraudulent Cottingly Fairy photographs taken by two young girls, Elsie Wright and Francis Griffith. Their abilities lay not in discovering fairies but in trick photography and a skill for glueing wings to cut-out figures from magazines. This was, in hindsight, clearly indicated by the fact that the 'fairies' were impeccably up to date in the fashions of the time. Nevertheless, the point is that these phenomena were, and still are, taken seriously by some. Likewise, whilst mermaids might seem the stuff of Hans Christian Andersen fairytales, there have still been reported sightings in the twentieth century. This includes a sighting off the coast at my favourite haunted location of Sandwood Bay in Sutherland, which was made during the 1940s by a shepherd named Sandy Gunn, who also reported sightings of the more conventional ghostly phenomena for which the bay is famous.

If this chapter tells us anything, it is that ghost hunters do not quite know what they are actually hunting for. There is not just one type of ghost to find, but many types of tantalising phenomena that behave in different ways and drive those who are looking for firm patterns and tendencies wild with frustration. So not only are we trying to discover and prove (or disprove) the existence of something, we do not really know what that something actually is. The only thing conclusively proven is that ghost hunters must be people that love a challenge. If a challenge is to be taken seriously, it is important that the tools and techniques for surmounting it are carefully looked into. So, enough, of definitions, it is to these tools which we now must turn.

five

THE STRANGE ART OF GHOST HUNTING – PART I

Scientific equipment and how it should be used

I mentioned earlier in this book that there have been so many previous publications about allegedly haunted places, but so very few about how to find out whether they are actually haunted. With that in mind, it is perhaps not surprising that a vast army of enthusiastic and (on the whole) intelligent investigators often achieve little more than an amateur night of ghost tourism. Yet most of us at least strive for rather more than that.

In the UK, perhaps with the exception of one or two glossy spin-offs from television series', there has been little written recently about the practicalities of ghost hunting. Perhaps there have been no widely available books on the subject since Andrew Green's original *Ghost Hunting: A Practical Guide* (1973) and Peter Underwood's contribution in 1986, *The Ghost Hunter's Guide*. Some of the insights provided here are, of course, timeless; such as Underwood's analysis that a ghost hunter has to be a 'detective, investigative reporter, scientist and psychologist'. Such issues as the type of equipment used have, however, changed out of all recognition, as in fact have some types of phenomena. Neither of these two experienced ghost hunters, for example, had ever to that point experienced orb phenomena (small balls of light that normally appear on digital cameras and which some say indicate the material which constitutes a ghost). In the meantime, a whole selection of new and affordable equipment has become available for investigators of all levels of experience and competence. I claimed though in the last chapter that we do not even know what ghosts are. If this is the case, how can we be sure if we are measuring their presence, whether it is with high-tech equipment or with traditional methods of investigation? This is the true riddle that faces investigators whether they are new or experienced. But without recording devices (including the eyes and ears of the investigator), there would be no investigation at all. It is therefore essential that this riddle is at least partially solved.

The other problem that an investigator faces regarding equipment is that the belief pattern of individual groups of investigators will affect what equipment they believe a ghost hunter should use. I ended Chapter Three with quotations from a survey carried out amongst investigators. This emphasised a fundamental difference between those who investigate using only scientifically tested techniques against those who investigate using equipment and experimentation not yet proved by science. The former category includes such equipment as thermometers, cameras and EMF meters. The latter includes the use of mediums, dowsing rods and planchettes. This chapter will concentrate on equipment that is regarded as scientific. What I hope to do is to look at each piece of individual equipment that a ghost hunter uses, assess its usefulness and its drawbacks, and ultimately whether it should take up valuable space in a ghost hunter's 'kit bag'.

Even though we are first looking at those measuring and recording devices whose workings are already agreed within science, science has no agreed opinion as to:

🪶 *How they should be used in a potentially paranormal environment.*

🪶 *When any results should be thought of as 'significant'.*

🪶 *What any 'significant' results would actually mean.*

Whilst the recent evolution of high-tech equipment, replacing the mercury thermometers and cine projectors used by classic twentieth-century ghost hunters, has undoubtedly made the whole scene appear more scientific, how many ghost hunters really understand the theories behind what they measure?

Any list of equipment should begin with the most talked about device at this point in time, this being the EMF meter.

The EMF Meter

Some investigators even casually call this a 'ghost detector'. With an audio buzz in many models accompanying the change in EMF frequencies, the temptation is surely there to nervously whisper to colleagues as the buzz gets louder, 'I think I've found a ghost'. Let us, however, call an EMF meter by its full name, which is electromagnetic field meter. It is a device designed for measuring electromagnetic fields at various frequencies; nothing more, nothing less. I mentioned in Chapter One that electromagnetism was discovered in 1825 by British inventor William Sturgeon. It is, of course, a well-known phenomenon caused both naturally and by man-made devices. With such a background of electromagnetic fields in the environment, the first key mistake many investigators make is to carry a hand-held device. The device in this case would be expected to pick up different levels of EMF for perfectly natural reasons as it moved around the room in the hands of the investigator. Taken away from the controlled environment of a fixed point in the room, any results would be next to useless during an investigation. It can, however, be used in this way prior to an investigation to sweep the area for any existing EMF hotspots.

The problem with the way in which EMF meters are used in investigations also goes much deeper. This is because there is (at least to the best of my knowledge) no real theory on how, and if, electromagnetic fields would vary at the point of a paranormal event occurring. In fact there is a working hypothesis that electromagnetic fields, when present for non-paranormal reasons, trigger effects on the brain that could make it more susceptible to interpreting a natural event as a paranormal one. The parapsychologists W. Roll and A. Nicols have done a good deal of research on this. In their aptly named report 'Psychological and Electromagnetic Aspects of Haunts', they tested a number of allegedly haunted sites and found that the naturally produced, underlying levels of electromagnetic fields were higher than expected in a majority of cases. Thus when a researcher's EMF meter starts to 'twitch', it may in fact be giving a natural explanation for a strange occurrence, not detecting the paranormal in action. So a (non-hand-held) EMF meter potentially remains a useful tool for the ghost hunting kit. Its function, ironically, is as a potential ghost debunker rather than as the ghost detector so many had thought it to be.

There is one further fundamental flaw with many EMF detectors in that they were not designed for paranormal investigations but simply to record EMF that may be given off by domestic electrical appliances. In the UK the level given off by appliances is around the range of 50Hz, whilst the range thought to perhaps impact on the human brain is between 0.5–30Hz. Most EMF models in use are therefore not calibrated to measure the range that they need to measure. Yes, an EMF meter should go into an investigator's kit bag, but it should be chosen with care.

Cameras

Unlike the EMF meter, the camera has been in use for well over 100 years in the investigation of the paranormal. However, despite its length of service, the significance of the result gained is very debatable and mainly subjective. We often smile now at the more obviously fraudulent spirit photographs from Victorian times. It may however surprise you somewhat to know that even more than 100 years later there has been no collaborative effort by those involved in paranormal investigations to get any form of agreement as to when a photograph is of 'interest'. One investigator's photograph of a 'mysterious entity' can be another's 'strap over the lens'.

We would have hoped that by now that there would be some well-grounded, scientifically objective way to define the anomalous from the mundane in conventional photography. With camera manufacturers apparently uninterested in sharing their expertise however, it is certainly not available to the researcher to date. Thus, photographic evidence seems to add to the confusion rather than clarify the outcome.

The number of photographic anomalies and the debate regarding their nature has increased massively since the advent of the digital camera. They tend on the whole to fall into two distinct types:

- *Orbs – the most famous phenomena that seems to have arrived with the age of the digital camera. These could be described as small, floating, transparent balls of light that some claim are the 'building bricks' with which a ghost is formed.*

- *Mists – a transparent mist, which sees to hover over the camera when no mist was present at the time. While less talked about, these are sent almost as frequently to the Spontaneous Case Committee of the SPR as their orb counterparts.*

When investigating photographs taken by digital cameras, however, the first thing of which any investigator has to be aware (unless he or she has taken the photographs) is the ease with which they can be doctored by any photo editing software after the event. This is unlike conventional photography where the original negative can always be referred to. The risk of doctoring can be lessened if the original memory chip from the camera is made available, but as this is normally necessary to keep the camera functioning, photographers rarely volunteer to send this. When using digital photographs in research, the fraud hypothesis can thus rarely be fully explored. This also means, of course, that it can be rarely be fully rejected, which in itself makes digital photographs a rather unsatisfactory medium with which to work.

Setting this objection to one side however, orbs had certainly become the new great hope for proving the paranormal at the turn of the millennium. Most groups visiting a typical haunted place on a large, set-piece investigation were virtually getting them to order. This caused great fascination, not only amongst ghost hunters, but also the press and television at the time. However since then there have been several independent investigations as to what the phenomenon of orbs actually is. Philip Carr, a colleague of mine during my time on the Ghost Club council who is also a skilled photographer, researched the matter at some length. He produced both an article and a very informative video on the subject which basically came to the conclusion that orbs were caused by particles of dust which interact on the digital mechanism, particularly of cheaper cameras with a lower number of pixels. He stated that:

> If any of these particles are caught by the flashlight of a compact camera at the moment of exposure a few millimetres from the from of the lens, they will be intensely illuminated, extremely out of focus, and rendered as balls of light or 'orbs'

Note that the general need for flashlight and dust explains nicely why such things occur more frequently in the old, dark, dusty houses that are so often the focus of investigations.

His research is surprisingly similar to a standard letter produced by a major camera manufacturer, which attempted to explain the phenomena. It explained in summary that:

> Because digital cameras have a greater depth of field compared to 35mm Cameras, such things as small dust particles and droplets of water drifting close to the camera are within a digital camera's field but not normal 35mm cameras. Normally these particles are very small, but when a flash is used the dust particles or water droplets are illuminated and are extremely obvious on the picture taken.

At about the same time, Steve Parsons, the energetic and talented researcher from Para.Science (whom I mentioned at some length previously), was also researching the subject. His amusingly titled internet article 'Orbs, or a load of balls?' hints that he came to roughly the same conclusions.

I have spent a fair amount of time on orb research simply to show that what was once a potentially compelling piece of photographic evidence for the paranormal has, through careful research, been shown to be, on the balance of probability, something entirely different. Some paranormal groups still take orbs seriously, but unless there is something particularly compelling or different about the orb on your photograph, I would not currently recommend that in itself it constitutes paranormal evidence.

Perhaps because of the controversy surrounding orbs, research into many potentially paranormal photographs involving 'mists' have been largely ignored. Within the Spontaneous Case Committee of the SPR, it has been postulated that they could be water vapour on the lens when a camera encounters sudden changes in temperature, for example between a warm car and a cold, dark house. As yet, no research has been done to prove or disprove this and therefore the 'mist'-style phenomena remain of interest.

Does all the above controversy mean we should discard the trusty camera from out kit bag after over 100 years? In my opinion this should certainly not be the case. Visual records are most important and the imperfections of each system (conventional and digital photography) can be overcome by ensuring both types of camera are used on an investigation. Whilst a conventional camera is far less open to manipulation, both of the deliberate and atmospheric types, with a digital camera it is far easier to take a high number of photographs which can be more easily sent to colleagues to analyse. By using both types of photography, weaknesses in either can be overcome and any phenomena common to both would be far less easy to argue away.

Thermometers

The traditional mercury thermometer has been a mainstay of a ghost hunter's kit ever since the early to mid-twentieth century. That said, there is no specific theory, at least to the best of my knowledge, to explain why temperature should drop when a paranormal phenomenon occurs. What there is though is a general hypothesis amongst ghost hunters that if the production of supernatural phenomena in some way uses energy from the atmosphere, this could possibly lead to a drop in temperature. This would work in perhaps the same way as a refrigerator does. What is much more important than this hypothesis, however, is the fact that through the long history of ghost hunting there have been enough incidents of temperature drops, both perceived and recorded, to make this something that is well worth testing. Some haunted places are even famous for having a 'cold spot' in the vicinity of the most haunted room or area. In fact, most ghost hunters would, metaphorically speaking, feel half-naked without one. There is consequently no reason why they should not remain part of any ghost hunter's kit.

There does, however, remain the decision of what type of thermometer to take. Many 'paranormal' stockists and some television programmes have encouraged the use of infrared thermometers, usually combined with a laser for target spotting. These will be better recognised by the man in the street as 'thermometer guns', which can be aimed at a particular spot to record the temperature of that area at that time. Now there is surely something very satisfying about going to a haunted house and firing a gun-shaped object around the room to try to 'catch' a ghost. Whilst satisfying it may be, scientific it is not. There are two specific reasons for this.

Firstly, even the general hypothesis on the nature of paranormal temperature drops would refer to energy being taken from the environment. These infrared thermometers measure the temperature in relation to a specific surface area. They are in most cases jazzed-up catering thermometers designed to measure the temperature of foodstuffs. This would be ideal if you were investigating a haunted hamburger, but of very little use in real-life paranormal situations.

Secondly, we are not trying to measure temperature for its own sake but temperature change, which may indicate paranormal phenomena. Even with the best aim in the world it is very unlikely that a paranormal investigator at three o'clock in the morning will aim his thermometer gun correctly at exactly the same spot every few minutes to give a proper account of temperature fluctuation.

These devices do have some use in some pre-investigation preparations as they can measure naturally cold surfaces in a room (e.g. an air conditioning duct) which could, in some instances, give clues to natural reasons for temperature fluctuation during an investigation. However, as a main temperature-measuring device to be used during an investigation they are somewhat dubious to say the least.

The main thermometers in our kit should therefore be of a more low-tech variety. They should, of course, be digital, as analogue thermometers are notoriously inaccurate and hard to read correctly, especially in an instance where a room is not properly lit.

The ideal type in my opinion is a digital min/max thermometer which, as well as reading the current temperature, also stores the minimum and maximum temperature for the particular session of an investigation. It can thus show clearly how varied the range has been. Another particularly useful device if a haunted area is to be kept free of people is a static thermometer which sends an infrared signal back to its own digital display, allowing temperature to be measured remotely. This is, of course, an entirely different principle to the infrared thermometer guns we discussed above.

Even with the right equipment, it is worth noting that there is no generally agreed formula for when a temperature change is to be regarded as significant. As a guideline though, look for quick, sharp drops. Several degrees Celsius over the duration of a couple of minutes, for example, is unlikely to be caused by normal cooling in a room. It would therefore be good practice, should a possible paranormal event occur, to immediately check all temperature measuring equipment.

Finally, thermometers should of course be kept in a fixed spot and not moved during an investigation. I have seen at least one instance of a tired, though otherwise well-experienced, paranormal investigator pick up a thermometer to record the temperature and look in awe as the temperature rose in his warm hand!

Tape Recorders

Tape recorders are another long-time stalwart of the ghost hunter and their basic method of use is thankfully, for a change, not the subject of any major debate. The logic behind them is simple. Ghosts, and particularly poltergeists, can sometimes appear to make audible sounds. If those sounds are recorded, and if there is no clearly plausible explanation for those sounds, the recordings would provide at the least *prima facie* evidence of the paranormal. The possibility of recordings providing good evidence for the paranormal has actually been increased recently with the experimentation by Barry Colvin of the SPR on paranormal-type rappings which I have briefly mentioned before. To recap, his provisional findings as recorded in the journal of the SPR indicate that paranormal knockings (a key phenomena since brought to the attention of the public by the Fox sisters in the nineteenth century), start with a low resonance of sound and gradually peak. This is in contrast to normal knockings (for example, banging the wooden desk I use to work on with my knuckle) which start as you would expect with a high resonance of sound and gradually diminishes just like an echo. If this theory stands up to further scrutiny, there will be a method of testing, at least in the cases of rappings, whether they are potentially paranormal.

Other types of possible paranormal sounds that are recorded still have to be validated by common sense and detective work. Footsteps, for example, are difficult to validate unless everyone in a building can be meticulously accounted for at that time. (This is a key argument for an investigation not being too large and unwieldy.)

With some unusual noises, however, it is just impossible to reach a certain conclusion. I co-organised an investigation some years back in the actively haunted Jacobean mansion, Charlton House in Charlton, East London. A loud bang was heard and recorded in one of the rooms occupied by an investigation team. Most of them clearly stated that the sound came from within the room; however at least one member was adamant that it was a firework from outside. This was a quite plausible explanation considering the investigation was in October, not too far away from bonfire night. More interesting still was that the views on the noise roughly split along the belief patterns of the investigators. At the time, those claiming an internal source had in the main a belief in the spirit-led explanation of hauntings and were possibly psychically gifted. The minority but equally credible view came from someone with a scientific background who could be described as an open-minded sceptic. At the time it was not really possible to find a sound expert sufficiently capable of bridging this divide. Indeed, there is still an acute shortage of such acoustic experts today who will risk their credibility testing such things. This is another reminder of the importance of co-operation between paranormal investigators and the scientific community. Despite occasional shortcomings such as this, a tape recorder remains a key tool for the investigator. Such a tape recorder:

- *Should be mains operated and only run on batteries when essential, so as to help it function at a constant speed.*

- *Should be a full-sized variety and not a dictaphone as otherwise copies will be very difficult to make.*

- *Should be a dedicated tape recorder and not a radio cassette. This takes away the possibility of the device inadvertently recording via its own radio receiver.*

At this point, it is also worth mentioning a very different type of phenomena that can be picked up on tape. Up to now we have been talking about a tape picking up and recording unusual sounds, which would also have been heard by witnesses in the room. It is claimed by some, however, that paranormal entities can talk directly onto a tape. This is a phenomenon known as 'electronic voice phenomena' or EVP.

Efforts were made as long ago as the 1920s to find ways of directly recording paranormal voices, both by the well-known psychic researcher Hereward Carrington and by renowned inventor Thomas Edison. However, it was only during the

1960s that research, initially from Swedish filmmaker Friedrich Jurgenson, brought this possible phenomenon more attention. After tape recording strange voices accidentally, possibly including those of his dead mother, Jurgenson spent five years further researching the subject and published his findings in a book, *Voices from the Universe*. This research was replicated and taken further by Latvian psychologist Konstantin Raudive. Using his own techniques he managed to record voices directly to tape which he claimed were from the dead. He published his findings in 1971 in a book called *Breakthrough* which indeed truly brought the theory of EVP to both his parapsychology peers and a wider public audience.

The phenomenon of EVP remains actively investigated to this day and certainly has its supporters in the paranormal research community. Others, however, think it has a rational explanation. The 'voices' only normally come in short spurts with poor grammar and a rhythm very unlike normal speech. Even more significantly, the voices sometimes only construct sentences in polyglot (a mixture of different languages), and other messages have to be slowed down or reversed to be understood. This starts to sound a little like the false accusations in the 1970s and 1980s that certain heavy metal rock bands were passing on demonic messages which could only be heard if the record was played backwards. This phenomenon was actually an example of a non-paranormal psychological trait known as apophenia, which is the brain's tendency to try to make sense and find patterns in things. In the case of rock's demonic messages, the sounds in question were random musical and vocal noises being interpreted as meaningful speech. Could not EVP be another example of this? Raudive, for example, spoke several languages and thus could interpret such noises as polyglot speech. Others who do not speak more than one language tend to find the meaning in their mother tongue. I myself find this explanation quite compelling. Another equally compelling natural explanation for other types of EVP phenomena is the ability of ordinary electrical equipment to sometimes pick up short pieces of radio broadcasts.

While it may well be that EVP can be explained naturally, this has not yet been done conclusively. It is still therefore worth checking from time to time to see if there are any direct messages picked up by your recording devices, even when nothing has been heard.

Camcorders

Unlike still photographs, there has been far less analysis as to the workings of a camcorder in the production of anomalies. This is perhaps because there have been far less examples of 'strange things' appearing on a moving image. It is nevertheless useful to have a camcorder as a record of an investigation. It is also scientifically valid to use a camcorder to point to a paranormal 'hot spot' for the duration of an investigation. In such an instance however, one should first take a judgement as to just how 'hot' a spot this is. Remember after all the poor, dedicated member of your team who will have to volunteer to go through hours of footage from the same camera angle. A camcorder chosen for any purpose on an investigation should obviously be able to operate in low light.

Night Vision Scopes

The necessity or not of these in any investigation depends, not surprisingly, on whether the investigation is to be carried out partly in darkness. The use of darkness as a catalyst for generating phenomena is a controversial notion which we will talk more of later. In some circumstances, however, darkness is inevitable. Examples of such circumstances would be an open-air location, which is investigated after dark, or when investigating mediums feel more comfortable operating without light. We talked at some length about the Scole mediums that were investigated by an SPR team in near total darkness (see Chapter Two). Imagine the insight that could have been gained had a night vision scope been used there.

This brings us to what might be a moral dilemma for some investigators. Should such apparatus be used clandestinely? An investigator may suspect a medium of fraud, a house owner of faking phenomena to get attention, or even a member of his or her team of indulging in childish behaviour. Under such circumstances, is it legitimate to use night vision without forewarning? My answer to this would be a qualified yes. However, if the night vision equipment showed the opposite of what the investigator was suspecting, he should, in most instances, explain with tact what he had been doing and include the night vision evidence in any report.

Night vision monoculars tend to be the right size for any investigation. The ideal one should not have a great deal of magnification included, as most investigations will involve it being used in close proximity. It should, however, have some kind of infrared light source to allow use in total darkness. On a final practical note, some of the more sophisticated varieties have small LED display lights to indicate on/off. Should there even be a possibility that the monocular may be used clandestinely, a model without such lights should of course be chosen.

Barometers

I know most readers may initially get an amusing picture of a ghost hunter carrying around a big wooden box with an arrow which points to either 'Sun' or 'Rain'. Most barometers today, however, are digital and compact. The other thing that is important to remember is that barometers do not measure changes in the weather, but changes in air pressure. Air pressure affects the weather, but can also affect so many other things as well. Such effects could extend as far as strange knockings and ear popping, both of which could be interpreted as paranormal. Just like EMF meters, barometers do not detect ghosts but indicate a change in the environment, which may trigger off a 'paranormal-type' experience, which can ultimately be explained naturally.

Motion Detectors

Simple electronic motion detectors can be useful, both for securing a particular part of a site from fraud and giving warning of the start of an outbreak of poltergeist activity. Based on any theories we have at the moment however, they are unlikely to be triggered by any paranormal entity itself.

Infrasound Detection

The final piece of high-tech equipment that, in my view, warrants detailed explanation is an infrasound detector. In theory this would be of great use to a ghost hunter, except for the very important problem that such equipment does not come in an affordable kit form to date. It is, therefore, unrealistically expensive to most ghost hunting groups. As normally seems to be the case, one of the few exceptions to such investigative limitations comes from the Liverpool-based Para.Science group. Para.Science not only has access to such devices but, in 2006, developed its own version of an infrasound detector called ARID (Acoustic Research Infrasound Detector). These were used in their exhaustive Camel Laird shipyard investigation in which unusually high levels of infrasound were experienced.

Infrasound, like EMF, is not evidence of a paranormal happening, but a possible natural explanation of something that may give a paranormal-like experience. Despite the fact that it is EMF detection that is all the rage (perhaps because basic detection devices are actually affordable), the evidence suggesting that infrasound can affect the way we perceive things is actually far more thoroughly researched to date.

Vic Tandy of Coventry University was very much the first pioneer of this theory. When working late one night in a laboratory that was supposedly haunted, he felt feelings of uneasiness and thought he saw a grey shape approaching him before it disappeared. Similar disturbances had happened in the past to the cleaner of the same laboratory, and the same thing happened to Tandy again the following day. What Tandy (who was also a keen fencer in his spare time) noticed during his second experience was that the blade of the fencing foil that he was keeping in the laboratory was vibrating. Upon noticing this, he wondered if there could be a connection. Tandy located a large extractor fan and through experimentation eventually discovered that this was causing infrasound, which in turn appeared to be causing the movement of his foil. He postulated that if such sound could have an effect on a metal foil, why not also on the human mind?

In fact, NASA had already conducted similar experiments in the past with infrasound, showing that at a frequency of about 18.9Hz, human eyeball oscillations could take place. With such an impact on the eye occurring, why then could it not cause optical illusions? Such a theory was backed up by the fact that when Tandy turned the extractor fan off, he felt that a huge weight had been lifted. From this initial experience, he went on to investigate this phenomena further, trying to find correlations of infrasound and paranormal-type experiences in various sites, with some success. His work was detailed in the two important papers he wrote on the subject, 'The Ghost in the Machine' (1998) and 'Something in the Cellar' (2000), before his untimely death at the age of fifty in 2005.

Of course, for such explanations of the paranormal to become truly scientific the results need to be replicable. There have recently been attempts to do just that. After their encouraging results at Camel Laird in 2006, the tireless Para.Science team grouped up with Ciaran O'Keefe (known to many from his television appearances in *Most Haunted*, but also previously a respected psychology and parapsychology lecturer at Liverpool Hope University). Together they set up a large-scale experiment in the underground museum cellars that are the remains of the now-covered slum street of Mary King's Close, Edinburgh. Mary King's Close is supposed to be haunted and is a scary place at the best of times. It had, as with many sites, some background infrasound but not at the accepted levels that would interfere with perception. With the help of an SPR grant, the team introduced infrasound-generating equipment to the Close. They would turn the equipment on some days and not others, asking visitors to the underground tunnels to complete a questionnaire detailing the experiences they had had.

While there were few, if any, examples of 'a white phantom jumping out at me and giving a blood curdling scream' type of report, in a more subtle way the results were reasonably impressive. Most striking was the fact that over twice as many people under the influence of infrasound had multiple strange experiences (strange in these cases included such things as feelings of being watched, anxiety, discomfort and nausea).

Infrasound is therefore definitely worth testing for. At the time of writing, I have heard of several efforts to produce a device that will test it at a reasonable price. Hopefully by the time of reading this publication, you will have the option of placing it into your ghost hunting kit – an option I would very much recommend.

Other High-tech Scientific Equipment

Some ghost hunters, especially in the USA, make claims as to the use of ever more sophisticated and expensive equipment. While none of these items are in any way unscientific, the use of more and more equipment in what may be a very unpredictable situation can result in what I have previously termed 'equipment fatigue'. Investigators, after all, are only human and given too many things to measure, may cease to measure those things properly.

Some ghost hunters, for example, claim that paranormal phenomena are 'known' to cause the surrounding air to ionise and thus travel with ionisation meters. There are also claims that high levels of electrostatic charge can encourage paranormal phenomena. Efforts therefore can either be made to measure such charge or even to increase it by way of a device such as a Van De Graff machine. We currently have many amateur ghost hunters, some who would even call themselves 'ghost busters'. However, based on these theories of electrostatic charge actually creating phenomena, the next generation of enthusiasts armed with such equipment could be known as 'ghost generators'.

On a serious note, I would not in any way attempt to diminish new attempts to explain the subject, but there can be as many theories as investigators. These particular theories are still very controversial (even relative to other theories of the paranormal, as all theories of the paranormal are, of course, controversial). Simply to keep the equipment used to a manageable level, I would not therefore recommend their inclusion in any kit as standard. If they are found to be relevant to a particular investigation they can always be added. A few ghost hunters in even more speculative moods suggest the use of a Geiger counter to test for radiation. This may have been an obvious thing to test in UFO cases, but I am unaware of any widely accepted theory which relates it to paranormal events originating on this planet. However, should such a device start to indicate radiation to a significant level – ghost or no ghost – it is definitely time to vacate that particular site.

Low-tech Scientific Equipment

We have added many new items of high-tech equipment since the days when Andrew Green and Peter Underwood were writing their guides on the subject. However, many everyday items of equipment still have a lot to offer the average ghost hunter. Such a ghost hunter may not always be scientifically trained and may feel more comfortable with technology that he is familiar with, along with the key ghost hunting skills of common sense, observation, deduction and an open mind.

Both writers recommend the following equipment in their books. While sounding basic, they still have important uses to this day:

- *Graph paper – to be used for drawing clear plans of the haunted site.*

- *Ruler or tape measure – this is, of course, for measuring distances. Hopefully this could be the distance that an object is moved on a successful ghost hunt.*

- *Watches – ideally these should be digital and viewable in the dark for the timing of events. These should be synchronised by each of the investigators.*

- *Voltmeter – this is for checking electrical power faults that may be the cause of 'ghostly' power cuts.*

- *Strain Gauge — this can be used both for measuring the force it would take to open a drawer or door, and for weighing the weight of an object that may have been moved.*

- *Magnifying Glass — this is (self-evidently) used for taking a closer look at any evidence.*

- *Transparent Envelopes — these can be used for storing any apports or unusual objects for further study.*

- *Flour — not to be used for cooking at some more remote locations, but an ideal and simple device for sealing off a room by sprinkling it in a large enough area that any intruder would leave footprints. We do have motion detectors for this purpose today, but the simple bag of flour is all the more efficient as it can differentiate between human footprints and, say, those of unwelcome rodents.*

- *Black thread — again this is useful for sealing rooms; in this case it must be used clandestinely to avoid any hoaxers replacing it. It has the advantage of encouraging hoaxers to stick to his or her normal behaviour pattern, thus uncovering the fraud. Such devices as flour or motion detectors would, of course, warn off a dishonest person.*

- *Torches — their use is self-evident in any ghost hunt that may involve an element of darkness.*

- *Candles — not necessarily for lighting, but useful to detect any air flows and thus provide an explanation for any cold spots.*

- *Whistle — this is for ending a particular part of a vigil when the ghost hunters are split in various parts of the haunted site. This can alternatively be used as a cry for assistance. Modern alternatives are two-way radios. However, reception cannot always be guaranteed and whilst looking more 'high-tech', they can be far more unwieldy when trying to operate whilst still using so many other bits of equipment.*

    ❧ *Detailed Ordnance Survey map – this may give clues as to the nature of the haunting; perhaps, for example, by showing that a farm is on the ancient site of a monastery (in the case of a mysterious ghostly monk).*

    ❧ *Chalk – can be used to make temporary marks showing the location of an object in case it has moved or, if very fortunate, to record where an object has mysteriously moved to.*

And last, but not least:

    ❧ *A good old-fashioned thermos flask and unbreakable cups – these should be unbreakable to make them easier to carry and because you never know when those pesky poltergeists might try to stop you from having your well-earned cup of tea.*

Both of our 'old school' ghost hunters make specific comments about the overuse of equipment, which I have earlier called 'equipment fatigue'. Underwood points out that:

> One ghost hunter I knew used to take with him over five tons of equipment yet, perhaps surprisingly, his reports were of no more interest to the scientist or anyone else than those prepared by an amateur with the simplest ghost hunting apparatus.

> (*The Ghost Hunter's Guide*, p.27)

Andrew Green, while reviewing a scientifically based ghost detector built by a leading member of the SPR, wrote that:

> It consisted of a camera linked to a tape recorder, linked to a photo-electric cell linked to a noise and vibration detector, a small electrical bulb, a sensitive wire circuit and a buzzer. The idea was that if anything made a noise in a room that had been wired and sealed the camera would automatically take a photograph... the tape recorder would be switched on and the light and buzzer would operate.

1 The Ram Inn, Wotton-under-Edge.

2 Inside the Ram Inn. The former pub is now a private dwelling and has escaped modernisation, retaining its charming atmosphere.

3 The Black Horse, Pluckley. The village is reputed to be the most haunted in Britain.

4 The author outside the Ferry Boat Inn, Cambridgeshire. (Dominique Fraser)

5 Chingle Hall. In the 1990s, this was regarded as Britain's most haunted house.

6 Ightham Mote. Tales link the house to the ghost of Dame Dorothy Selby, but the facts of the case suggest otherwise.

7 A view of 'Main Street' in the House of Detention museum.

8 An example of the misting effect on a photograph taken at the House of Detention.

9 The claustrophobic tunnels at the House of Detention, Clerkenwell.

10 The 'hanging man' exhibit at the House of Detention. Can the spooky atmosphere of a place encourage people to believe they have seen a ghost?

11 Woodchester Manor. (Copyright Woodchester Manor Trust)

Opposite from above

12 A gargoyle and eerie windows at Woodchester Manor.

13 Mysterious writing discovered on the wall of Woodchester Manor.

14 Elizabeth, Countess of Dysart, is reputed to haunt Ham House.

15 Ham House, Surrey. (Copyright Ken McKenzie)

16 Ardvreck Castle, Sutherland. This area is steeped in mystery, and it has been suggested that the veil between this world and the realm of the supernatural may be thinner than normal in such places. (Copyright Dominique Fraser)

17 Poenari Castle, Romania. This site is possibly haunted by Vlad Dracula.

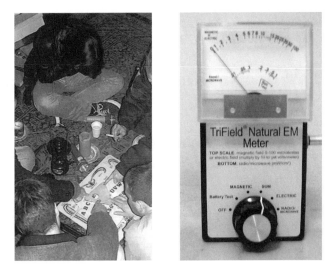

Left 18 Ghost hunters using a Ouija board.

Right 19 A Trifield Meter, one of many devices that can be used to take EMF readings. (Dominique Fraser)

20 A typical Ouija board.

21 A panorama of Sandwood Bay. (Ann Bowker)

22 Sandwood Bay. (Ann Bowker)

23 Crashing waves on the desolate beach at Sandwood Bay. (Ann Bowker)

24 There are many different places for ghost hunters to present their findings. Here, Alan Murdie, Ghost Club Chairman, presents a paper to a congress in Romania.

25 The site of Borley Rectory. (Eddie Brazil)

26 Borley Church. (Eddie Brazil)

27 A 'dust orb' photograph created by natural means. (Copyright Philip Carr)

But the problem was to decide on how sensitive the pieces of equipment should be. If it was too sensitive, someone sneezing in the next room for example would cause all the equipment to operate: the light would come on, the buzzer sound, the camera would flash and the tape recorder would start.

(*Ghost Hunting: A Practical Guide*, pp. 56-57).

In addition, I imagine all the equipment would have had to have been reset until the next ghost hunter sneezed again. This was an ingenious device undoubtedly, but perhaps just a touch too sensitive for field investigations.

There is therefore much scientific equipment a ghost hunter, even with limited resources, can take onto an investigation. The key is to take what is suited to the environment and the items the ghost hunter him or herself really understands how to use. If these rules are adhered to, a well-run ghost hunt can, at the very least, lead to significant conclusions for the participants. If it can be shown to be well run and well reported, it can also lead to evidence for those of an open mind that were not there. The equipment we have talked of in this chapter though is of course only half of the story. There are some apparatus and techniques which depend on either accepting some theories of the supernatural or at least suspending any disbelief for the purposes of using them and gathering results. Are such methods still valid in a twenty-first-century ghost hunt? This question is important enough to merit a chapter in itself.

six

THE STRANGE ART OF GHOST HUNTING – PART II

Non-scientific equipment, and should it be used?

Mediums

We saw in Chapter One how the start of modern paranormal investigating was largely instigated by the explosion of apparently gifted mediums performing their skills to incredulous Victorian audiences. It is in fact quite plausible to suggest that without this 'coming of the mediums', ghost hunting and other paranormal investigating would not have evolved in the way that it did. Yet today, many groups rarely use mediums and the core reason for the revival of ghost hunting is, in many cases, ironically taken away from paranormal investigations.

While I would not be so crass as to categorise mediums as 'investigation equipment', they are undoubtedly a resource on an investigation . What they also represent by their presence is a belief both that the 'survival' theory of the paranormal is at least worth testing for, and also that it could be possible to test for it by way of channelling paranormal communications through the subconscious minds of others. If the latter of these theories is rejected outright, we have no use for mediums on investigations. Nor do we have use for the whole selection of equipment designed to allow channelling through the subconscious for less psychic people who are unable to summon up a conversation from within by way of a few deep, trance-inducing breaths. Such equipment as Ouija boards, dowsing rods and planchettes would therefore be of little use if we rejected the use of the subconscious for channelling the paranormal, a concept that was largely discovered by mediums.

It is worth noting that before taking the decision whether to make use of mediums, you should take into account that there are several varieties of psychic skills to choose from (although each medium may possess more than one of these skills). These are:

- *Physical mediums – this type of medium produces phenomena that any person sitting with the medium can also hear or see. Such phenomena could be raps, audible voices, materialised objects or spirits taking a physical form from where they can communicate with the audience. Such phenomena is very rare now and when it does occur, it is usually only at private sittings. This means it is unlikely that a purely physical medium could be used in an investigation of a haunted location. Should an opportunity arise however, a sitting where such a medium was present would most certainly be worth an investigation in itself.*

- *Clairvoyants – this is the ability to see spirits or other paranormal images. Clairvoyants can do this either subjectively (picking up the images within their own minds) or objectively (actually perceiving the image through their own eyes). This ability is certainly of some use on an investigation. For example, the medium could see how a building used to look many years ago. However, whether this can be used as evidence does depend on the medium's ability to articulate the details of what they can see, and so other types of mediumistic skills may be of more help.*

- *Clairaudients – these are mediums who can directly hear spirit communications. Such a skill can be of particular use in an investigation as a medium does not have to articulate an image, simply report on what the communicator is actually saying.*

🐾 *Clairsentient – can sense the presence and the thoughts of a spirit. They are the ones that could sense a strange atmosphere in a room. Due to the subjective nature of such judgement, this skill is only of limited use on an investigation. However, clairsentients also have ability in psychometry (the ability to pick up information about the owner of objects from the object itself). This makes clairsentients very easy to test as the subject of their insights may well be alive and well, and very able to verify or discredit the observations.*

Why then do many investigation groups not use mediums? In some cases the reason for this is simply that a lot of mediums use their talents for professional gain. While there is nothing wrong with this in essence (we all have to use our talents to pay the bills), what it does mean is that a medium may also charge for out-of-hours paranormal investigations. This has a number of consequences.

Many paranormal investigation groups may simply not be able to afford the fees. Like the infrasound detector mentioned in Capter Five, a medium may be priced too high to be a viable resource. The Spontaneous Case Committee of the SPR was approached some years ago by a very genuine member of a spiritualist-type organisation who wished to start a series of experiments. It was difficult, however, to get sufficient members of the organisation with psychic abilities to commit their time unpaid, and the initiative never really got off the ground. This is not meant to be a criticism of the organisation, who were very much in principle willing to bridge the gap between psychics and researchers, but simply shows that people who use their gift quite openly to make a living have a reluctance to do unpaid overtime. Would it be any different if they were doctors, dentists or teachers?

If a medium takes payment for an investigation, he or she may feel 'under pressure' to perform, to give what would be in essence his or her clients some 'value for money'. It could therefore be suggested that any results gained were not gained with a truly open mind. If a medium agrees to work for nothing, in the medium's eyes they are often doing the researcher a favour. After all, mediums are normally confident as to their abilities and may feel no desire to investigate them further. What this usually means is that if a medium is offering services for the benefit of others, he or she may be prone to requesting any investigation is conducted on their terms. The SPR's Scole experiment was an excellent example of this.

So even if a ghost hunter wants to work with a medium, they can be quite difficult to obtain and use in a way that fits with the rest of the investigation. The gulf between psychics and ghost hunters runs deeper though, in much the same way as the chasm between ghost hunters and parapsychologists. Perhaps perversely, the main reasons for this are reversed. It is the ghost hunter who in some instances does not want to be seen as unscientific and the medium who feels that the investigator is there just to rubbish their claims.

If we are to be honest about it, neither of these suspicions are groundless. Many of the early paranormal investigators did have great suspicions of mediums, and since the nineteenth century many mediums have been shown to be little more than a cheap stage acts. Virtually all of the early photographic evidence for physical mediums has now been discredited as easy-to-spot double exposures or similar types of fraud or malfunction. Ectoplasm (the material that apparently came from a medium's body and which entities used to take on a physical existence) was shown in several cases to be remarkably similar to fine muslin. It was, for example, pointed out by the *Oxford Companion to the Body* (Eds C. Blakemore and S. Jennett, 2001) that an example of ectoplasm produced by the medium Helen Duncan 'even had stitching around the edges'.

It is undoubtedly true then that some high profile mediums have been caught cheating. This may be just a minority, but it is a significant enough minority to make at least some researchers treat them with suspicion. This suspicion can be reinforced in the slightly peculiar way that many clairaudients work.

If you have ever witnessed a clairaudient tackling a large audience you will have seen the tendency of some of the mediums present to fish for information. Pointing to a large table of twelve, the medium may ask if the name George means anything to them. On seeing blank stares, the medium may state that the name is actually Geoff (then perhaps Gertrude or Gillian). I am perhaps making a parody of the situation, but a tendency certainly exists to 'fish' for a name that is recognised by a sitter. The entity may start as someone's father and then become a grandfather if there is no recognition in the first instance. It may well be claimed that contact through to the realm of spirits is not always of the clearest quality, but the messages only seem to be unclear with regards to very specific facts and names. When the spirit talks in general terms, telling everyone it is happy and wishing them goodwill, there seems to be no problem with communicating. Now this type of performance can make all but the total believer suspicious. These suspicions may not necessarily extend as far as fraud, but it may be that the medium is looking subconsciously for clues. As (for example) groups of old ladies are far more likely to be seeking to talk to an Albert or Ethel rather than a Samantha or Shane, such names are 'heard' in the back of the medium's mind. This, of course, is just a speculative hypothesis and one piece of research that really needs to be done with mediums is not just to test their performance, but to try to compile descriptions from mediums of exactly what their experiences are when they perform. Is the 'audient' experience in clairaudience the same as hearing external sounds? If not, how is it different? Why are certain parts of communications so clear and others not? Are the spirits not willing to give out certain information, or are other spirit voices interrupting?

I know of no such specific work done to date to interview a large cross-section of mediums to try to understand what they experience in non-psychic terminology, and also to see if one medium's experience is similar to the next. Recently, however, some of these types of questions have been tackled in a fascinating book by the parapsychologist Ciaran O'Keeffe and medium

Billy Roberts called *The Great Paranormal Clash*. The book takes the form of a friendly 'jousting match' between the two parties, and gives fascinating insight into the beliefs and rationales of each of the two sides of the debate. More cooperative ventures are undoubtedly required to stop the 'them and us' mentality that currently runs between supporters and sceptics of the mediumistic process.

Despite the fact that a significant number of spirit mediums have been exposed as frauds in the past, there has also been sufficient impressive evidence to stop mediums being pushed to the fringes of paranormal investigation. Every now and again you will find what appears to be a really good example of psychic communication which does not involve the clichés mentioned earlier.

I experienced such an occasion myself some years back, before my interest in the paranormal was as extensive as it is today. For this reason, I can tell you about it only in anecdotal form having recorded no details at the time, not even the medium's name. I was not on an investigation, but was simply out for a 'fun' afternoon one Sunday with my sister and a friend of hers at a sitting of the Spiritualist Union of Great Britain at their impressive premises in Belgrave Square.

Unlike subsequent mediums I have experienced, this one specifically chose the people who she had messages for. The messages and the people who were apparently sending them also seemed to have meaning to the predominantly elderly sitters. Towards the end of the session, the medium pointed towards our little group and apologised for having so few messages for the 'younger' members of the audience. She explained this very credibly by adding that we had far fewer loved ones on the other side. She then added, almost as an afterthought, that she could see a maple leaf floating above our heads. This left my sister and her friend virtually with shivers running down their spines. The very next week they were off on an extended trip to Canada to tour the country and visit family friends. (Neither of them is the slightest bit Canadian, or would give off any clues to this connection.)

By any standards, this and the other comments made by the medium were impressive. In hindsight there are also two interesting observations about the medium's accurate comments about my sister and her friend. Firstly she made no claim to be communicating with any dead people and so her observation, if paranormal, would have surely been either a straight-forward premonition or ESP. (These are explanations that mediums usually frown upon compared with the past life explanation. You may remember from my discussion of the Scole experiment that Maurice Grosse was actually banned from participating for making such a suggestion.) Secondly, the imagery used was fascinating and further justifies my suggestion that us non-psychics really have to try to have a greater understand of what mediums experience. She was not simply getting knowledge of the future, or even for example picturing my sister visiting the Niagara Falls. She was actually claiming to see a symbol of the future (a floating maple leaf). Was this simply colourful language on her part, or an actual sighting? If the latter, who or what did she think produced this symbol? In hindsight, it would have been a great idea to have asked, but then again it was only meant to be a 'fun' Sunday outing.

In the same way as we were totally baffled by the revelations of our medium, there are just enough mediums throughout history that have also performed impressively to keep at least a realistic possibility alive that their gift is a paranormal one. The best example of a medium unexposed by sceptics was the physical medium Daniel Dunglas Home (1833-1886).

Home was possibly illegitimate and a sickly child who was adopted by his aunt in Portobello, Scotland, before later moving to America. He grew up at the time of the Fox sisters and appeared to have far better developed gifts. These gifts led to his eviction by his aunt, who believed his rappings to be the result of possession. Home, however, was meant for better things, and went on to lead the sort of existence that had not been seen since the times of John Dee many centuries before. He was ultimately to spend his time moving in circles of royalty and fascinating them with these talents.

In addition to his skills as a physical medium, Home could also levitate. He first demonstrated this in the house of an important American manufacturer, Ward Cheney. In 1855 he moved to London and demonstrated successfully to the famous names of that time such as Lord Lytton. An attempt on his life then followed in Florence by a local who feared his strange powers, before he was summoned to the French Court of Napoleon III who was also apparently convinced by his abilities. By then these included table lifting and the materialisation of a hand with a deformed finger, which the Empress recognised as that of her dead father. Although Home never accepted payment for his demonstrations, he was undoubtedly looked after by his ever growing band of noble sponsors. He even married into Italian nobility in 1858.

The most vigorous testing of Home was to come in 1871 by the eminent scientist William Crookes (who was later to become President of the Royal Society). To the surprise of many scientists, Crookes found the phenomena to be genuine. Home did seem to operate in an entirely different way from most mediums of that period, complaining himself about fraudulent mediums in his book *The Lights and Shadows of Spiritualism* (1873). He also could not understand why other physical mediums worked in darkness when he did not.

As a final twist, he lived for ten years after his death was initially (inaccurately) reported in 1876. This was more to do with the inadequacies of the French press rather than supernormal powers. He finally died in France in 1886. Whilst fifty-three was not such a grand old age, for a child who was initially thought too sickly to survive he had by then had a profound impact on the world and on paranormal research.

Home's story is an important example of a number of mediums whose abilities have remained genuinely unexplained. This is all the more significant as he operated in ways that seemed to discount all the obvious ways of fraud. There are other examples of this through the twentieth century. In the 1970s Mathew Manning, initially the 'victim' of a strong poltergeist phenomena, then discovered he had paranormal powers of his own which included automatic writing and the drawing of new pictures remarkably close to the style of dead artists. He became a major paranormal celebrity of that decade before settling down to becoming a more conventional psychic healer, which he remains to this day.

Despite the undoubtedly chequered past of many mediums and psychics, there are enough of them who remain untarnished to still take the phenomena seriously. If the psychic's ability is even possibly genuinely paranormal, then why not use it in ghost hunts, at least in principal? In the same way as you do not have to totally believe in ghosts to investigate them, you need not totally believe in the ability of psychics to use them on an investigation.

At the outset, however, both the psychic and the investigation's organiser would first have to agree guidelines as to the style of their involvement together. Such guidelines could state that:

- *Psychics and mediums should ideally be taken 'blind' to haunted premises, assuming the site is not well-known. This means a psychic will only know the general area he or she is heading to and will have no opportunity (accidentally or otherwise) to pick up information on the haunting by conventional means.*

- *Ideally, more than one psychic should be used independently. This is more practical if psychics are shown the 'haunted' premises prior to any investigation. If one psychic corroborates the evidence of the other in their observations it would be particularly impressive.*

- *During an investigation, etiquette must be agreed upon to ensure a psychic does not interfere with the investigation's other aims. For example, the psychic's observations should perhaps only be reported to one member of the group to stop auto-suggestion from others. There is nothing like a graphic report, for example, of seeing 'the drowned lady on the staircase shivering with cold' to send a very real feeling of shivers down the spine of all those who climb the stairs. Alternatively, if such a phenomenon is identified by a psychic during an investigation, there is certainly an argument for redirecting people and equipment onto that staircase to see if anything is recorded or felt.*

In short, the medium should compliment an investigation rather than dominate it and in most circumstances it should be clear that it is the location that is being investigated and not the medium. This way the medium is under no external pressure to get results. While it is normally distracting to try to investigate a medium at the same time as a haunted house, if there is a suspicion that the medium is consciously taking information from natural sources, it is possible under exceptional circumstances to test out this suspicion. It was fairly widely reported that just such a series of tests occurred in a national television show some years ago when a medium was reputedly fed on the identities of non-existent people, and then received messages from, or became possessed by them.

The point of this example is not to make claims as to the genuine powers, or otherwise, of any one medium. The point here is to show that the findings of mediums are, in fact, an easily verifiable form of evidence. Whilst, as I have previously said, such techniques should only be used in exceptional circumstances, when used they are the final element of proof that with planning, mediums can be used in a controlled environment. It would therefore simply be lazy rather than scientific to exclude their participation from investigations.

I have written in some depth about the use of mediums in investigations. This is because the other 'non-scientific' techniques we will now mention rise or fall on the very same theories that try to explain the ways in which mediums work. If, just for a minute, we accept that all the apparatus I will mention do in fact work on a paranormal basis, they can all be seen simply as ways of amplifying paranormal messages to those (such as myself) who are not psychically gifted. One such piece of apparatus though still manages to conjure up even more controversy that the use of mediums themselves. This piece of apparatus is the Ouija board.

The Ouija Board
Never has such an innocent looking piece of smooth wood caused such reactions (sometimes for, but more often against) from paranormal researchers. One of the chief books on the board is actually called *Ouija: The Most Dangerous Game* (by Stoker

Hunt, published in 1985). Now I doubt you would ever find a book entitled *The Dangers of EMF Meters* or even *The Dangers of Dowsing Rods*. Is this piece of equipment actually dangerous? Or is this just a modern myth, perhaps fostered by those of religious inclinations who object to it on theological grounds? Just as importantly, does it actually work as a way of gaining potentially paranormal information? And where does this information come from?

The Ouija is actually a very ancient invention. As long ago as 540 BC, the Greek scientist Pythagoras was renowned for using a similar device with his colleagues. In this case, the board was a table on wheels which moved towards symbols with the philosophers interpreting their meanings. Such traditions continued through to ancient Rome where, in the third century BC, the unfortunate soldier Theodosius was executed when Ouija board diviners proclaimed him to be the next Emperor. (Surely this is evidence itself of the danger of Ouija boards, even for non-participants.)

There were several other occasions in history where the use of Ouija-type instruments were to be recorded. The instruments recognisable to us, however, were to emerge in more recent times in two distinct varieties. The planchette was invented in 1853 by the French spiritualist M. Planchette. This differs from the more modern version of the Ouija board as it has a rolling pointer which, rather than pointing to a symbol, holds a pen, which it is hoped will write words or symbols.

The Ouija board itself (named after the French and German for 'yes' i.e. 'oui' and 'ja') was patented by William Fuld in 1892. The patent was later sold in 1966 to the children's games manufacturers Parker Brothers, who successfully sold it as a 'toy' that at one point outstripped the sales of Monopoly. There are various versions of the board today but a basic variety will consist of a smooth-surfaced base, normally of wood, on which there are printed the letters of the alphabet, numbers and the answers 'yes' and 'no'. Some varieties also feature the words 'hello' and 'goodbye' for the spirit who wishes a session to end, and '£' and '$' signs for the more materialistic spirits. In addition to the base, the board should have a smooth-running pointer, similar to a planchette, but without a holder for a pen. This pointer should be lightly touched by one or more people and may appear to spontaneously move in response to questions by participants.

There are basically two types of theory as to why the pointer or planchette should move. These are:

- *The spiritualist theory – there is (as we have repeatedly seen) almost always a spiritualist theory for most aspects of the paranormal. Such a theory states that all Ouija information is channelled from an outside source, which is invisibly moving the apparatus. Spiritualists would usually claim this to be our dear departed; others would add to this the possibility of elementals or even demons making communication.*

- *The automatistic theory – this was first suggested as a rational explanation for table rapping by the famous nineteenth-century scientist Michael Faraday. It can however be equally applicable to the operation of a Ouija board as accepted by most psychiatrists. It states that all information gained from a Ouija board comes from within the group. The Ouija board can therefore only access the answers the participants already have in their minds, either consciously or subconsciously. The planchette would then move guided by the subconscious muscle spasms of one or more operators.*

Use of the Ouija board continued to be popular and relatively uncontroversial throughout most of the twentieth century. It has been speculated that it was only after the release of the film *The Exorcist* in 1973, that people started to believe that a Ouija board could 'possess' the user, as was the premise of the film. Until then most people considered the channelling of Ouija information to be benign. This change in perception seems to have led to the reporting of all kinds of stories relating to the dangerous nature of the board. We will discuss the truth, or otherwise, of such dangers in a moment.

I have always been open-minded to all approaches of investi-gating the paranormal. The most commonly accepted assumption in ghost hunting is that spirits, should they exist, are no more evil or otherwise than the average man in the street. Therefore the only danger in investigations would then be if participants were ill-equipped to deal with the discovery of the unknown. Because of this belief I have never had any dogmatic opposition to Ouija boards, and have occasionally used them in set-piece investiga-tions. This has perhaps been more in hope than expectation, but also has had the advantage of keeping an investigation team alert in the early hours when continual thermometer-watching may well have sent them to sleep.

At this stage I will clarify what I mean by set-piece investi-gations. These investigations are not in people's living premises but in places such as stately homes, castles and caves. They are not cases where we have been asked to investigate because the ghost is causing anxiety, and where the purpose of such investigations is to hopefully reassure the owners, but places where the owners have no strong opinions about their ghost and which the ghost hunter has politely asked to investigate. As a Ouija board may cause (rationally or not) people's fears and anxieties to increase, they should never be used in this type of investigation where people are already scared.

It is fair to say that the few times I have introduced Ouija boards to an investigation the results have been basically meaningless. The 'best' results have included picking up the communications in the ancient basement foundations of an insurance company build-ing in central London where the spirit of the wife of a Reginald Fox communicated fairly clearly, even giving the name of a street in Hatfield where they used to live. This street, however, did not actually exist! This session also gave one of the more experi-enced participants a minor fright as the communicator accused her of knowing where her husband lived. This fright though was quantitatively little different to an investigator 'feeling an invis-ible hand (apparently) touching them' or 'hearing unknown footsteps approaching'. Ghost hunting is meant to be a little scary, and scary things are in no way the equivalent to dangerous things. Another time a Ouija board was tried in a deserted cottage once frequented by a military man. Here the word 'legions' was picked up repeatedly. This could have either been referring to the army legion which he belonged to or as a 'Hammer House Of Horror' style reference to the legions of devils mentioned in the King James Bible, Mark 5:9, 'And he asked me what is thy name? And he answered saying my name is Legion for we are many'. This reference to the Devil is fairly well-known and as I stated in my report at the time it 'was completely in keeping with our collective unconscious creating what we would expect from Ouija board in an old dark creepy house'.

So the Ouija board has hardly set my paranormal investigations alight with evidence, but then again many investigators will carry a tape recorder around for years without picking up the slightest unusual noise. So it cannot simply be the lack of effectiveness that causes the controversy. If it is not the Ouija boards possible limitations that makes it controversial, it must surely then be its perceived (or real) dangers. This makes opposition to them somewhat paradoxical in that if they can pick up 'dangerous' spirits, then this is certainly something any knowledgeable and experienced investigator could justify investigating! If, however, they only pick up the collective subconscious of the group, then why the big fuss?

In his book *A Lawyer Presents The Case For The Afterlife*, Victor Zammit wrote about the Ouija board's potential dangers. Let us look at his arguments and the possible responses. Zammit states in his book that, 'Psychic Investigator Archie Roy likens using a Ouija board to the practice of picking up a total stranger in the bar and inviting them home.' Taking the spirit theory of the Ouija board, this metaphorically is definitely valid. However, is it really as bad as it sounds? After all, the practice of taking someone you've only just met home from a bar may not be seen as savoury in a politically correct world. It is though something that has become a part of life since the 1960s, normally amongst younger adults with (rarely) any ill effect. This may sound a little flippant but if we are assuming that the contacts from the Ouija board are from the dead, the clear point worth making is that they are no more likely to be bad or evil than the average man in the street.

Zammit also points out that, 'No sceptic has been able to explain how groups of normal descent people have elicited horrible blasphemies… in a way that they certainly did not get from other methods that were supposed to project the unconsciousness'. This is perhaps a slightly unfair accusation as I know of no one, sceptical or otherwise, who has been asked to provide such an explanation prior to this time. Personally, I believe a potential explanation for this is quite simple.

First, take the continual bad publicity (in the media and horror films) that the Ouija board has had over the past four decades. Add to this the innate human desire for being mischievous and naughty (you will find an example of this in a game of Scrabble where players often disproportionately find 'naughty' words to use on their slate of letters). When you take both these factors together and assume that the Ouija board predominately picks up the subconscious of the users, it is hardly surprising that some of the board's communications can be of dubious taste. I mentioned an example earlier of a Ouija board session conducted by myself and other members of the Ghost Club, in which the 'entity' mentioned 'legions' in a way as to possibly identify itself with the Devil. There was in this instance no evidence of an evil presence to accompany the message, which would have seemed therefore to be a good example of what could be termed this so very human 'Scrabble board effect'.

Perhaps most important is the argument Zammit makes for evidence of harm done to Ouija board users. Here, Zammit refers to the writings of Hugh Lynn Cayce (son of the famous psychic Edgar Cayce), and the particular belief Cayce had that thousands of patients in mental institutions were there because of their dabbling with Ouija boards.

This sounds like damning evidence indeed until you start to wonder where these thousands of cases actually are. Would such a large number not have produced countless documentaries and human interest news stories? Would governments not be banning these evil boards in the same way as they ban mind-altering drugs? Or is this claim of 'mass insanity through Ouija boards' just a modern myth?

Alan Murdie, author, and Chair of the Ghost Club certainly thinks so. Writing on the subject in the club's newsletter (Autumn 2008), he points out that:

> The view that Ouija boards are in some way dangerous only seems to have grown up since the mid-1960s… rather like rumours of Satanism and black magic cults, stories of harmful Ouija board experiments have entered into popular folklore and horror fiction. Solid examples – i.e. those with names, places and dates and corroborating evidence are hard to come by.

I would tend to agree with these conclusions and feel there is a current lack of first-hand evidence as to the board's excessive dangers. To exclude what in essence is just a lump of polished wood from an investigation, solely on danger grounds, would be excessive in a discipline that is supposed to be all about the cutting edge study of new frontiers. However, while there is no reason to exclude this, is there any practical reason to include it? Does it have a valid effect, or is it just a distraction on an investigation?

A surprising supporter of the effectiveness of Ouija boards (for communicating with spirits) was a J. Godfrey Raupert, a leading member of the SPR in the early twentieth century. Raupert made a surprising and reluctant supporter because he was a devout Christian as well as a paranormal researcher. In his book *New Black Magic and the Truth About the Ouija Board* (1919) he condemns the board as being a 'Return to distinctly heathen and anti Christian beliefs' (p. 234). He however acknowledges earlier in the book, on p.216:

> That while much Ouija or Planchette writing is automatic and natural, intercourse with the spirits is and can be established by these means. Difficult as this conclusion may appear to some minds, it is nevertheless certain, that in view of the abundant evidence, any other explanation would present greater and indeed insuperable difficulties.

He does however also point out that, 'It has never been found possible to conclusively identify the particular spirit communicating'
(p. 216). He bases this on the sound theological grounds that the
facts which lead the sitter to recognise a spirit as a loved one must
be facts that the sitter knows and which 'are therefore accessible
to and at the services of a spirit invading the passive mind' (i.e. a
mischievous impostor).

If, however, Raupert is accepting that there is every likelihood
that these spirits are not what they claim to be, then surely by
using 'Occam's razor' the simplest explanation is not one of 'mischievous impostor spirits' (whose existence is only speculative)
but rather one of the 'mischievous subconscious mind' whose
existence has certainly been proved and who is certainly as capable as any spirit of invading the conscious mind.

Zammit, while mainly a critic of the board, also tries to defend
its powers to communicate with spirits by referring in his book
to the particularly impressive 'Patience Worth', communications.
These happened in 1912 when a lady called Pearl Curran received
Ouija messages from 'Patience Worth', who had lived in the mid-
seventeenth century in Dorset. Through the spirit of Patience,
Pearl Curran produced various very publishable books and poetry
which won national competitions. However, one of the books was
a long and historically accurate account of the life of Jesus. This
leads us to wonder how Patience, a female in the seventeenth century, would possibly have had the knowledge of ancient Roman
and Jewish life? Surely the more likely explanation again is that
Pearl's unconscious was doing the creating? It therefore seems
increasingly unlikely that Ouija boards directly communicate
with spirits. What is more likely is that they channel the collective
subconscious of the sitter or sitters. However, this should not in
itself be underestimated. If it can produce award-winning poetry
or long-forgotten information, it would be beyond our normal
understanding and so literally speaking be a 'paranormal' event.
We will see in our next section on 'table tapping', a similar channelling technique to Ouija boards, that subconscious channelling
in itself is enough to apparently produce poltergeist-type phe-

nomena. So even though there may well be no spirits to talk to, the Ouija board has the potential to produce some phenomena. It should therefore be an option on an investigation, but perhaps used sparingly simply on the grounds that some otherwise very good investigators find the whole thought of using it either objectionable or just too scary. There should, I believe, be three simple golden rules to its usage :

- *Never try to persuade an investigator who is genuinely afraid or wary of the board to use it.*

- *Never use it where the owners of a 'haunted' location are already in fear.*

- *Never ask overdramatic questions. For example if you ask the board if the communicating entity committed suicide, there is a near certainty the answer will be 'yes'.*

If these rules are followed a Ouija board can have a back-up role to play in investigations. As well as the experimental reasons for its usage mentioned above, it still has one very practical role. At 3 a.m. in the morning when nothing paranormal has happened, the distraction its use provides can ensure our intrepid investigators do not all fall asleep. Such a distraction in itself should not be underestimated.

Table Tipping

We have spent a lot of time discussing the use of mediums and Ouija boards, as the arguments for and against them rather encapsulate the variety of other 'non-scientific' ghost hunting techniques. All these techniques involve using the subconscious minds of either the sitters or mediums who will either communicate with spirits or communicate forgotten knowledge with the conscious mind. The only difference between these techniques is in their effectiveness and reliability.

Whilst the technique of 'table tipping' (an amateur séance) is rarely used today it does have a fairly good record of producing phenomena that appears to be at least paranormally based. It initially emerged in Victorian times from groups of people who were interested in spiritualist phenomena but either had a mistrust or a lack of financial resources to employ a medium. Table tipping is a simple technique needing no equipment other than a (fairly light) table upon which each of the investigators should lay their hands flat with the palms down. Questions can then be asked of the 'spirit' and if the technique is effective, spontaneous knocks or raps may be heard emanating from the table. The raps are often in the code (that seems to have been accepted by all disembodied entities) of one rap for yes, two raps for no.

If the technique is working particularly effectively the table can even move or lift off the floor. It is, however, a practice that has been known to work better after several sittings, and so may be of limited use in a one-off investigation. Perhaps not surprisingly, phenomena have been shown to be more effective in darkness or near darkness, either because it produces the right atmosphere for the spirit-type phenomena, or because it makes pranks and fraud easier. More surprising is the fact that recent investigations have shown that it is all the more effective when the participants are light-hearted or even jokey. This is in contrast with the solemn mood in which it was assumed that early séances should be conducted.

The nineteenth-century scientist Michael Faraday distrusted the spirit communication theory behind the phenomenon, and invented a table which aimed to discredit this notion. This was a table with two tops divided by a layer of ball bearings and rubber bands. When sitters worked with his device, the upper table top moved by itself. This showed that the sitter's hands were apparently moving the table, albeit probably subconsciously. The experiment did not fully explain the other phenomena behind table tipping such as the table raps and the table lifting into the air, and this technique still remains of some interest to the investigator.

While a conclusive natural explanation has not yet been discovered for table tipping, the theory that it was caused by discarnate spirits did receive a large setback in the early 1970s with revelations from what became known as the 'Philip Experiment'. The experiment was conceived by the well-known poltergeist investigator Dr A.R.G. Owen of the University of Toronto to test the notion that poltergeist-type phenomena did not come from external spirits of ghosts. His group collectively devised a fictitious character called Philip, inventing the full details of his life including a wife named Dorothea and a doomed mistress called Margo (she was ultimately burned at the stake). It was deliberately meant to contain all the over the top features that many historical ghost stories seem to contain. After some months of experimentation, 'Philip' started to contact the group through intelligent rappings in table tipping experiments. He very helpfully confirmed all the facts they had made up about him. What was most interesting was that the actual rapping noises could not be explained and the table not only moved frequently (which could have been explained by Faraday's experiment) but also danced on one leg and sometimes levitated. The phenomena was actually filmed in a television studio which included, in this case, additional electrical disturbances to the lighting. This also showed quite conclusively that the phenomenon was centred around the sitters and not one particular place.

Some may find it disappointing that the 'spirit communication' theory took such a setback. It can and has been claimed that it could have been mischievous spirits reading the sitters' minds and pretending to be 'Philip'. While this counter-argument can certainly not be fully discounted, it does have a certain convoluted feel to it and probably would not fit the 'simplicity' criteria set by 'Occam's razor'. Personally, I do not look at this experiment as being such a setback for the paranormal, as it seemed to indicate that the existence of a power in the mind to move objects (i.e. psychokinesis or PK). That in itself is would be an amazing new discovery.

Table tipping therefore is a powerful, if somewhat unfashionable, tool of investigation. It can probably only be used as a small part of a long term investigation (due to the number of sittings often required to get phenomena). As with Ouija boards, it should not be used when its melodramatic nature is likely to scare the occupiers of any premises or, for that matter, any of your own intrepid ghost hunting team.

However, due to its successes it should never be fully discounted in an investigation. As it also seems to be a people-centred phenomena, it may well be worth a team of ghost hunters actually investigating the phenomena in its own right rather than as a tool for part of another investigation.

The Planchette

As mentioned briefly in the section on Ouija boards, the planchette is often thought of as simply being a variety of Ouija. In fact, the pointer which runs across the Ouija board is often called a planchette itself. However it is worth noting the slight differences in its use.

The planchette has perhaps avoided some of the bad publicity that generates fear around the use of Ouija boards. It is simply a small, triangular device which holds a pen on wheels for automatic writing, and so would not have been so camera friendly in Hollywood horror films. It is probably fair to say that the average person does not know what one looks like, so is unlikely to be intimidated by one.

Whilst this may be an advantage, its main disadvantage is that it takes a great deal more practice to get it working effectively. On a Ouija board it tends to be obvious what letter of the alphabet is being spelt out. Writing that emerges from a planchette (other than in very skilled and experienced hands) would send most five-year-olds to the bottom of the class. The pen on the planchette is designed to keep constant contact with the paper and so the spirit (or the user's subconscious) has to write in flowing, joined-up writing. This would be a problem for most of us consciously in these days of word processors. Needless to say when a script is nearly undecipherable, the subjective minds of the investigators can try to interpret a meaning when none is actually there. Like the Ouija board, the planchette is of some historic interest to ghost hunters and can be experimented with at 3 a.m. to keep investigators alert, but the results, unless particularly impressive, should not be taken too seriously.

Divining Rods

Divining rods are thin metal wires bent at 90° and held loosely in each hand. When they cross over (or in some cases move apart) it is claimed to mean that the target the user is seeking has been identified. Dowsing with divining rods has long been used in the discovery of water and other objects with a great deal of apparent success. This traditional technique has, however, only recently come into wide use in ghost hunts.

On the face of it, there appears to be detailed research by Tom Lethbridge in his book *Ghost and Ghoul* which backs the use of dowsing beyond just merely finding water. Lethbridge suggests that dowsers can tune in to various types of fields which, in turn, could possibly hold the strong emotions or impressions of a previous event. However Lethbridge was a believer in the non-intelligent paranormal and yet many current field researchers use dowsing as method of trying to communicate with an intelligent being – something that even its chief proponent did not think possible and, as far as I know, has no real theoretical basis.

There are two further practical flaws. Rods can only use a yes or no format for answering questions which is slow and tiresome. They are also only operated by one person. This means the pressure to please the audience must surely lead to a subconscious or conscious desire to 'perform'. Having observed them in use on quite a few occasions, the information gained is often contradictory and meaningless.

Makeshift dowsing rods can easily be made by cutting and bending metal coat-hangers. Personally I would keep the coat hanger intact and use it to hang up my coat on an investigation. In my opinion this would be a better use of the resource. You will guess from the above that I do not recommend taking divining rods on a ghost hunt and suspect, like crop circles and 'orb photography', that they will be a passing fad of the paranormal.

There is a great deal of equipment that does not use the currently agreed laws of science. They are all very much based on the principal of channelling messages or energy through or from the human subconscious. Where these messages come from is still a matter for debate, although the survival theory in this instance sits a little uneasily with some of the facts.

It would be narrow-minded for either ghost hunters or scientists to decline to use these techniques because they are unsure if and how they work. When we deal with the paranormal we are unsure as to if and how anything works. We cannot just use current science to deal with 'para-science'. That would surely be unscientific. I have accepted that there are sometimes practical problems with using these techniques in investigations. When these practical problems are not applicable, or can be overcome, these techniques still very much have their place.

seven

THE STRANGE ART OF GHOST HUNTING – PART III

Organising investigations and avoiding pitfalls

Suddenly they started approaching him out of the mist. Some he recognised, some were strange faces he had never seen before. There was so many of them! Did they know why they had come, what their role was that night? Some were hungry and cold, and they all seemed to ask so many questions. They grew closer – surrounding him – draining the energy from him. This was the first time the ghost hunter had felt true fear... the time that he met his new investigations team!

The opening paragraph of this chapter might just exaggerate the problem a little, but anyone who has even attempted to organise an investigation will know that it is a potentially daunting event. This is especially so in larger, set-piece investigations (briefly outlined in the last chapter), in which up to forty participants have been known to attend.

The challenges of organising an investigation have always existed but have become more intense in the last decade due to the renewed interest in the subject. Most fair-minded organisations have a gut instinct to be as inclusive as possible, and as these organisations have grown larger, being inclusive has often meant bigger investigations, sometimes with fewer experienced investigators. Is chaos inevitable as ghost hunting becomes more of a mass participation interest? Or is it simply a question of ensuring that some timeless golden rules are adhered to?

In previous chapters I have tried to carefully analyse the pros and cons of equipment, techniques, and the reality of the phenomena themselves, hopefully arriving at a balanced and open-minded conclusion. In this chapter I intend to be far more dogmatic and opinionated, as most of the issues are practical rather than paranormal ones. I have seen quite a few ghost hunts fail because these practicalities were not taken into account (including in some cases by myself), and dislike the thought of ghost hunters in the future wasting their valuable time and effort making the same type of mistakes again and again. Should you be a ghost hunter and disagree with any of the following observations, please contribute to this debate with a book, article or even correspondence with myself. But ask yourself truthfully, have you ever been on an investigation and part of the way through the evening wondered to yourself what the group of people you were with were trying to achieve?

The organisation of larger, set-piece investigations should, by their nature, be very different to the cry for help type of investigations in the private homes of people, and it is these set-piece investigations which will take up most of this chapter.

Let me first though say a little about the cry-for-help investigations. These, by their nature, cannot be carried out to any kind of strict formula, as you have the genuine fears of people to contend with. Firstly, if you are in a position to receive correspondence from the general public, I would recommend that you use a common sense vetting criteria, as over half of this correspondence will clearly come from pranksters or people that the balance of probability will tell you are deluded. Assuming you are not a trained psychiatrist, this is not something even the best ghost hunter is equipped to fully deal with. Correspondence that you may not wish to follow up on could include entertaining e-mails like the one I received in wonderful deadpan style, where a correspondent described how he had 'a hungry ghost who ate his sandwiches every night'. I have also received less humorous examples of correspondence that perhaps should not be followed up, such as graphic and detailed descriptions of molestation by an incubus or succubus (mythological, sexual predatory ghosts). However, no specific type of alleged phenomena should be off limits, and the litmus test should be to ask yourself if a type of phenomena was happening to yourself, how would you try to describe it to others?

If the way the description is put over in correspondence is outside of the boundaries that you consider to be normal, then the chances are that the witness would have the same impression on you. Even if the witnesses outlook on things is the correct one (and he does, for example, actually talk to hobgoblins every night at the bottom of his garden, as he ever so calmly told you in his letter) there is little you can do to help, as your belief system would be far too removed from his to investigate objectively.

Any initial contact should be with no more than about three people, ideally including both sexes. Two burly ghost hunters turning up at the door, even if initially invited, may be intimidating to an old lady or an unmarried mother with young children.

It is essential that you make clear at the start that you are an investigator and not a 'ghost buster'. Also essential is to clarify whether the residents wish anonymity in a case. This should, of course, always be given when requested.

Any first visit should primarily be fact finding. Relevant witnesses should be interviewed, ideally recorded with a tape recorder, and the premises should be inspected for any signs of a normal explanation. If a subsequent investigation is called for, the nature of such an investigation must be discussed in detail and agreed with the occupiers. If the occupier feels uncomfortable with some angle of the investigation it should not be carried out. After any investigation, if the phenomenon remains unexplained it is important to also do your best to offer the help and reassurance that was sought. In some cases an explanation that ghosts tend to be harmless should suffice; in other cases, options such as a Church exorcism could be discussed but not specifically recommended.

One case that I investigated involved an unmarried mother who had been forced from her council home by an apparent entity. After being convinced that at the very least her fears were genuine, the help that we offered was very practical. We sent a copy of our report to the local council which was hopefully of assistance in the decision to re-house her.

Over and above these short snippets of general advice, cry-for-help investigations cannot be run to a set of rules, but by common sense, deduction and sometimes instinct. Much of this can only come through experience. For this reason the 'cries for help' should not be taken on by a group of novice ghost hunters, despite the temptation to investigate these often very active types of haunting. There are now plenty of other opportunities for people to get a grounding in the subject, and it is to these that we should now turn.

Set-piece larger scale ghost hunts are very much a modern phenomenon. Harry Price, for example, although he was President of the Ghost Club, appears to have never felt the need to organise large scale investigations for his members. He much preferred involving only his close and trusted colleagues, such as Professor Joad (who, as mentioned in Chapter Two, he famously platonically slept with in a haunted bed). Despite the fact that he rented Borely Rectory for a year, no large scale investigation by the Ghost Club or anyone else ever took place on the premises. Price preferred instead to invite a series of individuals to spend the night there and compare their observations.

Whilst the Ghost Club became more involved in investigating following the death of Harry Price, the number of participants on each investigation initially remained modest and manageable. The extended and well-known investigation into Langenhoe Church in Essex during the 1950s only involved six people. It was only in the 1980s that large investigations were really starting to occur.

The Ghost Club's 1988 investigation into 'the Rookery', a house in Downe, a village in Kent, consisted of no less than twenty participants in the one evening. Luckily my first investigation with the Ghost Club, although taking place one year after that of the Rookery, was a very well-organised affair involving only six people. As this took place in a haunted Lincoln bomber at RAF Cosworth Aircraft Museum, any further people on this cramped plane would have been detrimental to the investigation. Today however, large scale investigations of up to forty people are not uncommon. Ghost hunting colleagues of mine experienced an investigation fairly recently where they came across the strange sight of numerous paranormal investigators literally crammed into a corridor no more than 12ft long. Even the ghost must have been claustrophobic.

I mentioned in Chapter Two that ASSAP do run these large scale events partly as training exercises. In such a case, there is a legitimate reason for a ghost hunt being so large. Without such a reason, the ghost hunt becomes little more than ghost tourism, with too many people for the location to be properly controlled. I therefore strongly believe that no investigation, without exceptional reasons, should be of more than ten to twelve people.

If the above recommendation is accepted, the next step in organising an investigation is to find some method of deciding which twelve people should be selected. The Ghost Club currently does its investigation selections by lottery. This is, of course, done for the sake of being inclusive, but if a lottery fails to produce a balanced investigations team, it could actually exclude all those participating from being on an effective investigation. I remember the excitement generated from being invited on my first few investigations, and would not want to take that away from any potential new participant. I also remember my disappointment on arriving at some of my earlier investigations and discovering that nobody really knew what they were doing.

There are a number of key types of people that should be included in an effective investigations team:

The Investigations Organiser

Such a person should obviously be an experienced investigator. In addition they should have a good knowledge of the haunted site, ideally from a pre-investigation visit or, if this is not practical, by research. Prior to an investigation the organiser, even if representing a much larger society, should be allowed a reasonable amount of influence on who is attending the investigation. The organiser in turn has a responsibility to show his selections are inclusive. (I believe this balanced approach is scientifically termed 'common sense'.)

Prior to an investigation, the organiser is also likely to have to send a letter or email to the participants ensuring they know where they are going, what they need, what time they have to be there, etc. This may seem like stating the obvious, but only if you are used to doing such things, which not all investigators are. An experienced investigator that I have worked with in the past, for example, freely admits that on one of his early efforts at organising an investigation, due to communication problems, he accidentally left two of the participants outside the locked gates of a large old house, leaving them unable to participate.

The resources needed on an investigation must also be very clearly stated; an inexperienced investigator may assume that there is access to food and drink on a site when there is not. As many sites are in remote locations and are investigated late at night, such an omission can lead to a miserable experience for those concerned.

Likewise it also has to be spelt out what sort of clothing should be worn. This is not necessarily obvious when a location is named. The famously haunted Woodchester Mansion for example sounds like a sumptuous stately home. It is actually an unfinished Victorian folly, where only one of the rooms has any windows. The implications for not bringing the right clothing to a winter investigation in this location could actually be quite serious.

The organiser will normally have to make some kind of advance draft plan of who should be investigating where. This should of course be flexible, as the format of the latter parts of an investigation should be altered in response to any apparent paranormal happenings, or additional good ideas from the participants. Without such a draft plan it is very likely an investigation will descend into a free for all, with everyone doing their own thing.

To sum up, the role of an investigation's organiser must be very much one of a benign dictator. If the organiser is not effective in this role, the time to address this is not during the investigation, but afterwards when it may be suggested that the organiser's talents are better put into other parts of the investigations process. An investigation after all is never the right time to hold a committee meeting.

Because the organiser's role is so wide, varied, and in some cases daunting, another key role is the assistant investigations organiser.

Assistant Investigations Organiser

This can either be a formal or informal position. It is, however, very important, both for the stress levels of an organiser and the smooth running of the investigation, that the organiser has access to an experienced colleague that he or she both knows and trusts. Such a colleague should share in the responsibilities of running an investigation.

Many people bring equipment of varying degrees of sophistication to an investigation, and many societies now have their own equipment. It is surprising though, how relatively few investigators really understand how much of their equipment works – how for example photographic anomalies should be interpretated , or (as discussed in Chapter Five) what changes in EMF meters actually mean. For this reason it is important that every investigation has adequate cover for the role of the equipment expert.

Equipment Expert(s)

These are people on an investigation who have in-depth knowledge of most investigative equipment, and who should be able to give advice as to how it should be used and whether any results are significant. In an ideal world there should be two such people on any investigation. Even experts can interpret results subjectively, and if a consensus can be reached between two equipment experts, any results will be all the more impressive.

Such equipment experts need not be physicists, and due to the shortage of physicists amongst ghost hunters, getting two on any investigation would likely be impossible in any case. They need to be people who are familiar with working with electronic equipment, who can operate and take measurements in the near dark, and have enough understanding of what is being measured to know if any measurements are of significance.

Psychics

If we are ideally to have two people familiar with working with scientific equipment, we should also be even-handed and ensure that the more spirit-based theories of ghosts are also thoroughly tested. As with our equipment experts, there should ideally be two of them present. However unlike the equipment experts who should confer with each other during an investigation, it is best if the psychics are kept working separately. When this is done any similarities between the findings of the psychics can be most impressive, especially if this takes place in a building whose history is not well known.

Whilst psychics have an important use during an investigation, it can also be especially useful to take them into the premises prior to the investigation taking place. This means their findings can be recorded in a more controlled way, without either the distractions of other events, or the possible accidental feeding of information from other investigators. Alternatively a psychic can be used post-investigation (so long as they are not aware of the investigation's findings) to see if they can provide back-up for the investigation's results.

Other Members

A psychologist could give insight into what might trigger people's experiences in a dark, spooky environment. A rational, open-minded sceptic could provide a differing perspective on events. If the evidence is strong enough the sceptic will either change his belief pattern, or his counter-arguments will sound desperate and frivolous. Alternatively, if the other ghost hunters are getting carried away with every creaking floorboard, the sceptic can put matters in perspective.

In an investigation at Charlton House which I helped organise, a wooden mushroom-style ornament being used as a trigger object was seen and heard to have flown about 8ft in the air and came to the floor with a crash. Unfortunately, none of the participants in this subgroup of investigators had their recording equipment on at the time. However, the witness testimony of this 'magic mushroom' was particularly bolstered by the fact that the witnesses included an investigator who had always been openly sceptical about the paranormal. After that event he appeared to be sceptical no longer.

I have noted the types of people I think are key if an investigation is to be a success. Please note however that this is very much an investigations 'dream team'. A shortage of any of these areas of expertise would diminish, but not necessarily invalidate, an investigation. A shortage of too many of these skills, however, could invalidate an investigation and turn it into a piece of ghost tourism. It is also worth noting that whilst I have identified eight key investigations roles – the organiser, the organiser's assistant, two equipment experts, two psychics, a psychologist and an open-minded sceptic – in some instances it may be possible for an investigator to have more than one function. The psychologist could actually be the sceptic, the assistant organiser a psychologist, and so on. This would leave the way open for a larger number of newer, less experienced investigators to attend, who are of course the experts of the future.

Having a good strong team in place is, in itself, no guarantee of success. Just as important is finding the right place to investigate. The first key criteria for a good location may seem to be stating the obvious. This is to make sure the location you choose is actually a haunted one! This is not asking for you to be sure there are definitely ghosts there, which would rather kill off the point of an investigation in any case. There are, however, many old buildings that have a ghost story attached to them but have no recent evidence of any unexplained phenomena. Andrew Green noticed this when he wrote *Our Haunted Kingdom* (mentioned in Chapter Two). He excluded many famous hauntings from this book on the grounds that there had not been a sighting in the last twenty-five years. For our purposes this is perhaps a little generous, as a sighting every twenty-five years will, technically speaking, give our one night investigation only a one in 9,206.25 (including leap years) chance of getting any positive results. Whilst this is possibly over-exaggerating the odds (due to unreported sightings and the fact that not many people may stay at a location at night, when perhaps the chances of sightings are at the optimum) on the whole for a place to be worth investigating you would be looking for reports of activity within the last decade at the very least.

Secondly, make sure it is possible for a location to have an environment that is suitable for an investigation. The main concern here is to ensure that the premises will be relatively free of people, other than the investigators, and that any non-investigators who remain understand the nature of what you are trying to do. Particularly problematic here are haunted pubs.

Many pubs are renowned for having spirits other than those kept behind the bar and many of these also seem to have a fairly high activity ratio. This does not, however, make them worthy of an investigation in itself. Most set-piece investigations would normally take place on a Friday or Saturday night, to ensure that enough investigators are available. Pubs are open and normally busy until at least half past eleven at night and since the sensible relaxation of licensing laws by the government, this can be extended at the weekends. Add to this some clearing up time for the staff, and it may well be that the investigation will not start until after 1 a.m., with your team already tired.

Even at this stage the atmosphere may not be conducive to a good investigation. I have co-organised one investigation and attended another where the otherwise very friendly landlord totally misunderstood what we were trying to do, and let some of his favourite customers and bar staff remain watching and chatting at the bar. Remember that of course you are the landlord's guests, so you cannot at that stage insist that he leaves. It may seem obvious to all ghost hunters that a lock-in and a ghost hunt do not go together, but to those who have never seen a ghost hunt this is obviously not the case, and must be discussed in advance. Pubs are by no means an impossible place to investigate, but to say they can be problematic is an understatement. A ghost hunter will have to decide if the level of activity justifies the extra logistics, organisation and negotiation.

Hotels also give similar challenges for an investigation. One way around this, in the case of smaller hotels, would be to offer to buy up a proportion of the rooms at a time when the hotel is out of season, in return for exclusive use of the premises.

Any place of work that has a large night shift can also give significant problems. In such cases there may be no real way to overcome this and it may be impossible to hold a large set-piece investigation.

It is not only the nature of the location which will make an investigation difficult, the timing of an investigation can also be important. With our ever-extending firework festivities, any investigation during October and early November in an urban location can be interrupted by loud, disconcerting bangs. I have already mentioned an incident in an investigation at Charlton House where my colleagues were genuinely split as to whether a bang was an external firework or an internal poltergeist. In addition, it is important to make sure that an investigations team will be able to function effectively if an investigation is held during the coldest part of the winter. For example, I was genuinely concerned when some of my colleagues in the Ghost Club held a large investigation in mid-January in Woodchester Mansion, which is a shell of a building, open to the elements. Thankfully the weather was very mild in the end, but without that bit of luck the investigation may have been ruined.

Finally, make sure the location is a place where ghost hunters would wish to spend the night. This is not strictly speaking scientifically or logistically necessary, but takes into account the fact that you are dealing with volunteers who are giving up their time and want to have an interesting experience. A colleague of mine once brought me details of a genuine and active case involving a haunted traffic island. Even before the potential logistical problems were considered, this was immediately rejected on the grounds that we would look and feel plain daft spending the night there.

When choosing a location for a set-piece investigation, it does no harm to ask yourself that if no activity occurs, will it still be an interesting place to spend the night? All things remaining equal, a haunted castle may be preferable to a haunted office, and places which may consist of only one or two rooms give very little variation in a night's activities. However, when a location is very active such criteria for choosing a location will of course be set to one side.

Once a location has been identified and permission sought and hopefully gained, the one final issue that needs to be resolved is the timetable of the investigation. The key first question here is whether it is an all-night or part-night investigation (or if there is good reasons for it, a daytime one). I personally believe that all-night investigations, whilst they might sound impressive, are nearly always destined to fizzle out due to fatigue. They should never even be considered unless participants have somewhere to stay to catch up on sleep. I once attended an investigation at Chingle Hall, a reputedly very active premises near Preston in the north of England. The premises were very cold all night and sleep was impossible, with the result that I was in no fit state to drive the three or four hours back to London. Nearly falling asleep at the wheel, I was a danger to myself and my passenger. Thankfully I remembered that I had an old friend who lived in near by Macclesfield, and rested for most of the day there.

Since then I have came to the conclusion that an actual all-night investigation is as likely to result in additions to the spirit world as communications from them. In short, for anyone travelling they can be just plain dangerous! If a ghost hunt is to either go on all night or late enough so as the participants are unlikely to return home until the morning, it is essential that some kind of sleeping arrangements are made. This may only need to be a quiet area where people can lay their sleeping bags (which you as organiser would have told them to bring), but it needs to exist in some form or another.

Setting aside the dangers of an all-night investigation, you will find in any case that it is virtually impossible to keep momentum going much past 4 a.m. Fatigue will set in and assuming no extraordinarily significant results, there may even be an element of boredom. Records will perhaps cease to be kept quite as methodically by some of the participants. Most importantly, it will become near impossible for the investigation's organiser to keep the necessary concentration together both to organise a large group of people and try to make sense of what is happening in perhaps three or four different rooms.

Unless there are very significant results, I would recommend most investigations are completed by 4 a.m.

Even if opting for a part-night investigation, this can normally leave six or seven hours of investigative time to fill. The exact way this should be spent should of course vary depending on the premises and type of phenomena, but should include many of the following elements.

A pre-investigation tour by any psychics in your group
If this is done prior to others arriving it will ensure that the organisers have sufficient uninterrupted time to record what the psychics have picked up without neglecting the rest of the participants. It will also ensure that the psychics are not influenced (subconsciously or otherwise) by the other happenings during the investigation.

Familiarisation of the group with each other
In larger, set-piece investigations it is often the case that some people in the group are not well-known to others. It is important to make sure that a short time is spent familiarising everyone in the group. This can be done through each member introduc-

ing him or herself to the whole group in turn or even with
more informal ice-breaking games if the organiser feels confident with them. In a situation where there is a large number of
people who do not know each other, name tags could even be
considered.

Familiarisation of the group with the premises
It is important that at the start of any investigation all members of
your team tour the premises and familiarise themselves with the
layout. This will ensure they do not either get lost or go into any
areas which the owner has not given permission for the team to
be in.

Setting up of equipment
Equipment can either be kept in a particular room or travel from
place to place with an investigator. It is fine for devices such as
personal cameras, night vision enhancers and so on to be kept by
their owners. However, items such as temperature gauges, trigger
objects and EMF meters should be kept in a fixed position with
some means of recording measurement changes either electroni-
cally or manually. Such equipment should be set up before any
investigation properly commences, and careful records kept of
where each is positioned.

Rotating groups of investigators around the premises
This is normally seen as being the core part of an investigation.
A team is normally split into groups (of at least two participants,
and usually more) and each group is given a location to investigate
for a period of thirty-forty minutes. Notes should be taken of any
sounds, sights, feelings and smells whose sources are not immediately obvious. Each of the groups should then meet at base room
and refresh themselves before rotating locations.

   The extent to which the groups should publicly report their
findings at this stage is very much one for common sense. Minor
phenomena should perhaps not be publicly reported as it would
lessen the impact of another group reporting the same thing

later on. However a 'headless man' seen inside a wardrobe should be reported, as otherwise cameras and attention may not be on that spot.

Experiments involving the team as a whole
When a full rotation of sites has taken place, further experiments can continue using the whole group. The nature of these could depend on the results gathered previously. If bangs were heard consistently in one particular room, a séance could possibly be held there (if the group is suitably experienced in doing one) to see if any communications may come from the raps. During this time, recording devices in other areas can still be left running (preferably with the rooms sealed in some way).

Debriefing
At the end of an investigation there should be a discussion to try to make sense of everybody's experiences and any information withheld about the haunting to a team should at this stage be forthcoming. It is also very useful at this point to ask participants to put their general impressions in writing. An on-the-spot event report may only state that an unusual creak was heard at midnight. What you are interested in is who believed that creak to be invisible footsteps, and who was sure it was just the wobbly floorboard that they stood on earlier. Asking for written comments at this stage will get this vital insight.

At the end of the investigation, short of a phantom coach and horses galloping through the room, even the investigation organiser may not be totally clear how impressive or not the night's occurrences have been. The organiser will have a bundle of notes and be tired and fatigued. Only when it is possible for him or her to look at things with a clear head should an attempt to 'make sense of it all' happen and a final report be written. This stage is when the investigator becomes a detective and can be as fascinating as the investigation itself – as we will see in the next chapter.

eight

The Strange Art of Ghost Hunting – Part IV

Making sense of it all through research

Before preparing a final report on a haunting: believe nothing! Check and question everything!

I could end the chapter here, leaving you with the sense that the author has spent one night too many in old, dark houses and come out embellished with a sense of paranoia. This is in essence though all that this chapter really has to say.

This does not mean that you are accusing your team or the owners of the premises of cheating or fraud. You are simply accepting that human judgement and perception are both subjective and often not quite correct. Remember also that not to believe someone is not the same as disbelieving them. A good researcher is one that can get his mind into a sense of suspended disbelief, and let the facts do the talking unhindered by any preconceived ideas. Look at two imaginary but typical statements which clearly show the need to go through this process:

'Many people saw the grey lady in my manor house throughout the eighteenth century' said the sweet little old lady before giving you a cup of tea.

The lady here may be sweet and old (and her tea may be delicious), but she is not that old! How would she know what was seen in the eighteenth century? Yet she is speaking as if her knowledge was certain.

Likewise, if one of your colleagues states:

The strange line across the photo that I took in the haunted room was definitely not my camera strap.

Just how could he be so confident? All of the tens of thousands of photos of camera straps are taken by accident, so by definition no photographer would know when that accident was happening, and likewise they would be unable to say for sure when it was not happening.

The old lady's statement is nothing but hearsay, probably based on an extended multigenerational game of 'Chinese whispers' over the centuries. Your colleague's statement is simply a natural defensive reaction, an initial inability that most of us have to admit the possibility of making a mistake. Both their statements would need careful validation before being presented as facts in a report.

These examples were imaginary ones and perhaps you find it difficult to believe that they would arise in real life. Yet they not only do exist, they can be the whole basis on which a haunting is based.

On attending an investigation many years ago at the reputedly very haunted Chingle Hall near Preston, I was told by a local investigator (on hearing rustling from the stable block) that no animals were ever kept there. On checking it myself later, it was found to be full of cows!

A much more understandable error was made by a very experienced colleague of mine who had been asked by a television channel to assist in filming at Woodchester Manor. He was faced with an extensive array of apparently inexplicable phenomena, which would perhaps faze most ghost hunters. However, one of the phenomena he reported was faint writing appearing suddenly on one of the inner walls of the building. On checking with Woodchester's caretaker, however, we subsequently discovered that the writing, whilst faint, had been on the walls for many years. This type of understandable oversight can unfortunately lead to an element of doubt arising even when no oversight can be proved. On an investigation of a disused cottage near Ipswich for example, we were told that a mysterious footprint had only recently appeared when the house was locked. Whilst there was every chance this may in fact be true, taking into account that the average person does not specifically check for footprints every time they visit a house, there is also a possibility it may have been made before the house was secured.

Now perhaps you understand what I mean when I say, 'Believe nothing! Check and question everything'

The first and most basic check that needs to be made is to look at the internal consistency of the haunting both through the previous assumptions made about the haunting and through the findings of your investigation itself. In its simplest form, an imaginary case would perhaps consist of a ghost of a fifteenth-century nobleman shot in a pistol duel. A little historical knowledge here would immediately tell you that pistol duels did not exist in the fifteenth century and that the facts of the haunting must be incorrect. Again, for those who doubt such things can happen regarding real-life haunting, please see the next example.

In 1998 myself and (the then soon to be Chair of the Ghost Club) Alan Murdie were attempting to stay in Deal, Kent, just before Valentine's Day. Deal was the nearest town to the notorious Goodwin Sands. The tragic spectre of the ghost ship *Lady Lovibond* was reputed to have appeared on 13 February every fifty years since its sinking in 1748.

This once in a lifetime anniversary had been in my diary ever since I had been interested in ghosts, so we were disappointed to discover that the small town of Deal had become mysteriously fully booked around that date, not with courting couples but with ghost hunters from around the world wanting to catch a glimpse of the ship. This gathering of ghost hunters was prominently reported in the national press at the time. This mass interest in the ghost ship appeared rational as there had after all been apparently credible witness accounts on each of the other fifty-year anniversaries, and to add to this that the *Lady Lovibond* was a particularly tragic ghost story. It can be summarised thus. A quarrel broke out on the ill-fated ship due to the fact that the first mate was in love with the captain's wife. In a fit of jealousy the first mate drove the ship onto the Goodwin Sands, killing all on board.

An interesting and tragic haunting indeed and one which, because of the exact dates, I decided to check by gaining access to *Lloyds Register Of Shipping Wrecks*, a copy of which was obtained through my local lending library. I was disappointed not to find any record of the *Lady Lovibond* sinking. However I had entirely missed the point. It would have been most unlikely to have discovered any such ship, as the internal narrative of the haunting was inconsistent. Read the paragraph about the haunting again, and see if you spot the inconsistency!

The ghost hunter Peter Underwood certainly did, pointing out in his *Ghost Hunter's Almanac* (1993) that if all hands on board were lost, 'I have never understood how the story of the loss of the *Lady Lovibond* has been established in such detail'. How could all these dead people have narrated in detail this tale of love and tragedy? By its inner nature, the story of the *Lady Lovibond* has to be incorrect. The areas around Deal at the time were very much smuggling territory, and it is most likely that this type of ghost ship tale would have been an embellished version of one made up by smugglers both to explain late night comings and goings, and to give people a healthy fear of the area. Like all too many ghost stories, the *Lady Lovibond* falls into the category that I like to describe as 'ghosts that never were'; namely, famous ghost stories that have been proved false simply through research.

Of course, only a very limited number of ghost stories can be disproven or validated simply through the facts that are already at the investigator's fingertips. I have already mentioned how easy it is to order specialist, obscure publications to be delivered to your local lending library. A far more direct approach, however, is to glean information from sources local to the haunting. If the haunting is in a small village or historic town (as many hauntings seem to be), by far the best place to start is the local church. Not only is it likely to have a wealth of historical records of parishioners, but if your ghost is of a local person, it is likely that person could actually be buried there. If the ghost comes from a famous local household, such as the owners of a castle or a manor house, there is also every possibility that there will be a tomb, or even a private chapel, within an old church dedicated to such a family. This can all assist in checking out the ghost's supposed identity.

This technique though would surely be of little use when the supposed identity of a ghost was one that was bricked up in a local house?

Let us look to the most surprising case of the haunting of Ightham Mote, a beautifully preserved fourteenth-century manor house in Ightham, near Sevenoaks, Kent. It is commonly accepted that the manor house is haunted by Dame Dorothy Selby, who was rumoured to have been a key betrayer of the Gunpowder Plot. She is thought to have been bricked up at Ightham Mote for her deeds, and indeed the skeleton of a lady was found in a concealed cupboard in 1872. The haunting was mentioned in several ghost books in the 1970s and '80s. Although there is a shortage of recent sightings, Peter Underwood does mention in his classic *Gazetteer of British Ghosts* (1971) that several years previously a bishop failed to remove a peculiar chill through exorcism. (Bearing in mind that Dorothy Selby was a staunch Catholic, it was hardly surprising that she did not respond to a Protestant bishop.)

From the above account it would seem that we have an identifiable ghost, albeit one somewhat short on recent sightings, which is not in itself unusual. Unfortunately this was not the case, as a trip to St Peter's Church in Ightham would quickly reveal. Here you can see a large stone monument of the supposedly infamous Dame Dorothy Selby which clearly marks her date of death as being 1641. This is thirty-six years after the Gunpowder Plot, when she was of the ripe old age of sixty-nine. It also indicates her cause of death as the result of being pricked by an infected needle (while sewing). Despite this, several ghost books have appeared by respected authors which directly identify Dorothy Selby with the ghost of the 'bricked up' lady.

When an author is writing about over 100 haunted sites, one or two mistakes such as this can be quite understandable. However, if researching one particular haunting in detail, missing such a fact would be embarrassing. This is why such local research is invaluable.

As well as the local church, it can also be very interesting to talk to people at the local pub or perhaps post office. The landlord of a local pub would normally have heard most stories in a community and be able to give some indication as to whether they are taken seriously. A post office (if a community still has one) may give you the possibility of talking to more elderly residents from whom you could get a perspective as to whether a haunting is truly a historical one or a modern invention.

Much research seems to bring to light the fact that an original ghost story is unlikely to be totally correct. Strangely, however, this does not always mean that such a place is devoid of ghostly phenomena. Such a case in point is Ham House in Richmond, Surrey, a lavish seventeenth-century mansion on the banks of the River Thames. Ham House is supposedly haunted by Elizabeth Murray, Countess of Dysart, who reputedly murdered her first husband Sir Lionel Tollemache, to marry the Duke of Lauderdale.

The story goes that Elizabeth, in the form of an old lady, continues to haunt the place, tapping her stick in the bedroom and occasionally appearing. The first recorded, detailed account of the ghost was from the writer Augustus Hare, who apparently visited Ham House and recollected in *The Story Of My Life* (published in 1900) that:

There is a ghost at Ham. The old butler there had a little girl; she was then six years old. In the small hours of the morning, when dawn was making things clear, the child, waking up, saw a little old woman scratching with her finger against the wall close to the fireplace. She was not at all frightened at first but sat up to look at her. The noise she made in doing this caused the old woman to look round, and she came to the foot of the bed and, grasping the rail, stared at the child long and fixedly. So horrible was her stare, that the child was terrified and screamed and hid her face. People ran in and the child told what she had seen. The wall was examined where she had seen the figure scratching, and con- cealed in it were papers which proved that in that room, Elizabeth had murdered her first husband to marry the Duke of Lauderdale.

Augustus Hare, as you can see, had the art of telling a good ghost story to perfection. His writings are in many ways in the very same whimsical style as Elliott O'Donnell, who we discussed in Chapter One. Unfortunately it is very likely that the content was whimsical too. As the Ghost Club's research into this case points out, no mention was made of the house being haunted by any of the earlier known publications about haunted sites. This is of course surprising, as by then the ghost would have been two cen- turies old. A further clever bit of analysis from the Ghost Club points out both how unlikely it would be for a butler's daugh- ter to be offered accommodation in a room where the countess would have kept her private papers. The club's report also pointed out how unlikely it would be that any murderess would have kept such damning evidence in any case.

Charles Harper's *Haunted Houses*, written in 1907, only seven years after Hare's book, is perhaps more damning still in the criti- cism. He writes of Mr Hare's 'picturesque ghost stories', pointing out that Sir Lionel Tollemache had in fact died in Paris in 1669. As the countess was living apart from him in London during that time, poisoning would have been a bit tricky. He also points out that in any case the Duke of Lauderdale's wife did not die until 1671, mean- ing that the countess would not at that time have had her motive to murder her husband, so as to wed the already married Duke.

Even as early as 1907, Charles Harper was conducting the type of research that would do any of us proud. There is one further thing though to be learnt from this picturesque tale of the Ham House ghost; the great importance of discovering the original source of a ghost story. It is only through discovering the source that you can judge and test out the story's authenticity. If in the case of Ham House the original source is written 200 years after the event it describes, it is clear for that reason alone that the source will not be a reliable one.

There is however one final twist to the Ham House tale. Despite the fact that the original ghost story seems to have, in the main, been invented, there have been sightings of a strange, dark lady in the vicinity of the countess's bedroom, along with the strong, sudden and unaccountable smell of rose perfume, which I myself experienced on a visit. Has then a probably invented haunting somehow taken on a life of its own? Such are the wonderful paradoxes that a ghost hunter has to try to unravel.

My message in this chapter has so far been to emphasise the importance of questioning everything you hear about a haunting and suggest ways in which the true facts can be discovered. In summary, such methods can include:

- *Using the ordering service of your local library.*

- *Using the internet.*

- *Talking to (willing) locals, especially in communal places such as pubs and post offices.*

- *Visiting local churches, and other places where local historic records may be kept.*

- *Trying to find the original reference point for a ghost story.*

These can be interesting, though time-consuming, processes and below are a couple of tips on how it can be made easier:

- *The Society for Psychical Research has a service by which their journals of some 100 or so years can be searched via key words on the internet. As the SPR has existed throughout the history of modern paranormal research, this service is of great benefit.*

- *Many of the classic publications of ghost hunting have been republished in far more recent times, even if they may date back a century. They can therefore easily be owned without having to spend a fortune in antiquarian book shops.*

- *If the haunted site is at all historic, always purchase any guide books or local reference books as a matter of course. You will find that with regard to the site's history, most of the research has already been done for you.*

- *If the geography of the site is in any way important, always purchase a detailed Ordnance Survey map of the area.*

- *If you are able to publish your findings either on the internet or in some other form, it is always wise to include some way of allowing readers to contact you. You may find some extra background information this way or perhaps additional sightings of the 'ghost'. In this way, research into a haunting is very much an ongoing process.*

I mentioned at the start of this book a particular case that made me interested in ghost hunting. This was the haunting at the remote Sandwood Bay. Whilst my actual 'ghost hunt' may well have been just something of a personal challenge, subsequent research into this fascinating site was carried out in a far more painstaking way. The last part of this chapter will use this research as an example of the use of many of the suggested techniques above.

Location of alleged haunting: Sandwood Bay and Sandwood Cottage (overlooking the bay) in a wilderness area of Sutherland, Scotland.

Nearest major settlement: Kinlochbervie.

Identity of alleged ghost: Publications (in the 1980s) hinted at three possible identities of this ghost

Theory One: A Polish sailor (complete with uniform and beard).
The idea of the ghost being a long-dead sailor is the one which most accurately fits the sightings. As the same bearded figure has been seen both on the beach of Sandwood Bay as well as in the cottage, it seems a reasonable working hypothesis that the elements of poltergeist activity in the cottage may be linked to the apparition. Despite the sailor continually being referred to as Polish, there initially seems to be no evidence as to the sailor's nationality in reported sightings. There is no information as to which ship he may have been on, or evidence of witnesses hearing him speaking Polish. Indeed in one sighting he appeared to speak in very clear English.

Theory Two: An Irish sailor.
The hypothesis that the sailor is Irish ties in with one sighting only. This is a sighting in the early 1940s by local shepherds Gunn, Mackay and Macleod of a 'living' spectre that disappeared behind some rocks. I call the spectre 'living' as fourteen days later they claimed that a sailor killed when an Irish ship was wrecked was the very same man. While crisis apparitions (see Chapter Four) are a well-documented phenomena, there are no known cases of a crisis apparition becoming a fully fledged ongoing haunting. For this reason I do not particularly favour this identification of the ghost. It is also unlikely that the three men could have positively identified a brief sighting of the apparition with a potentially disfigured corpse, especially taking into account that both were bearded and thus hiding their facial features.

Both the 'sailor' theories perhaps needs to be adapted to simply being a 'long-dead sailor' of unknown nationality. This would be quite consistent with known facts as prior to the Cape Wrath Lighthouse being built nearby in 1828; the area had quite a history for shipwrecks.

Theory Three: The ghost is an Australian ex-resident of Sandwood Cottage.

This I believe is the least likely identification of the ghost. Its origin seems to have come simply from one passing comment made to the Scottish folk writer R. MacDonald Robertson by the shepherd Sandy Gunn after his experience in the cottage. Furthermore, according to an elderly local lady who I interviewed (who lived next door to Sandy Gunn's house and remembers him well), Sandwood Cottage was never inhabited by an Australian. There is also the question of course as to why an Australian resident should to all intents and purposes resemble a bearded sailor?

Reported sightings of alleged ghost:

Sighting One: In the early 1940s Sandy Gunn, George McKay and William Macleod saw a bearded man walk behind some rocks and disappear. Two weeks later they identified this man as being an Irish sailor who has since drowned in a shipwreck.

Sighting Two: In the early 1940s Sandy Gunn also once heard footsteps at night in Sandwood Cottage, and although he went downstairs to investigate he could find nothing.

Sighting Three: Spring 1949, two men from Oldshoremore were gathering wood when the 'sailor' told them to 'leave his property [i.e. the wood] alone'.

Sighting Four: On 8 August 1949, a fishing party saw the 'sailor' who disappeared before they could reach him. While they thought at first he was a poacher, the lack of footprints in the sand soon changed their minds.

Sighting Five: In July 1953 three visitors from Edinburgh saw the bearded 'sailor' on the beach. He disappeared, and when they went to the spot again, there were no footprints.

Sighting Six: Some time prior to 1961 an Edinburgh lady received pieces of wood from the broken staircase at Sandwood Cottage (none of which now exists). Various phenomena then occurred at her house. Crockery tumbled to the floor, there was a strong smell of alcohol, the wood occasionally rattled and she saw the ghost of a bearded 'sailor'.

Sighting Seven: Sometime prior to 1971 the fisherman Angus Morrison spent the night and saw a bearded sailor with peaked cap looking in at him through the window.

Sighting Eight: Some time prior to 1971 the same Angus Morrison was nearly suffocated by a thick, black mass that seemed to be pressing down on him.

Sighting Nine: In September 1970 walkers from Surrey decided to spend the night at the cottage and were awoken by crashes, bangs and heavy tramping steps for which there was no explanation. They reported this to the local postmaster the next day.

Sighting Ten: In 1986 some fishermen encountered a huge man in a long, black cloak who disappeared in front of their eyes in the direction of the beach.

Visit to site and locality, April 1988

The first thing to know when visiting Sandwood Bay is not to believe everything on your Ordnance Survey map. The map quite clearly shows a track leading to the bay, but at points this barely exists at all, while at others it is muddier than the heather that surrounds it. A normal car could then be driven carefully about two miles up the track with a further two miles to walk. For this reason it is important to ensure you have all essential items with you. After a preliminary trip, I had dinner in the Old School House restaurant just south of Kinlochbervie where I heard mention of an old hermit that frequently visited the cottage and who some people though may have been mistaken for the ghost.

Therefore, when I set off, I was both on the lookout for 'hermits' and ghosts.

I left my car and started walking to the house at about 7–7.30 p.m. With the lack of a track in the final stages and the fading light making navigation difficult, I only managed to find the cottage just as dusk was setting. This made me very aware that I could not navigate back until dawn. Initial checks for natural noises and sights in the area included floating white blobs on a nearby hill which I eventually identified as sheep. There was also an unseen light which seemed to intermittently flash on the wall of the house, which I deduced was the light from the powerful Cape Wrath lighthouse. The lighthouse itself was obscured by low mountains. I also found, unusually, that my tape recorder's new, high-powered batteries had mysteriously drained.

Despite the unique and somewhat unnerving atmosphere, nothing of any paranormal consequence occurred during the night other than an exhilarating feeling of awe of being alone in the wilderness in a very mysterious spot.

The next morning, on returning to 'civilisation', I visited the craft shop in Kinlochbervie where the owner was to prove most helpful. She informed me that:

- *The hermit I had been told about earlier really did exist, and was an old Glaswegian by the name of James MacRory Smith.*

- *That he did not actually inhabit Sandwood Cottage but a nearby bothy in better condition known as Strathchailleach Bothy. (This is clearly marked on the Ordnance Survey map.) He has apparently been returning there for the last twenty years, using it as his summer residence.*

- *That his description was well matched to that of the ghostly sailor, down to the bushy beard and the peaked sailor's-type cap which the ghost is reputed to wear.*

- *That the postmistress in Oldshoremore could likely give me more information.*

She also introduced me to some boat repairers in the next building who confirmed that the witnesses from the 1940s sightings had long since died. The search for the later witness, Angus Morrison (sightings seven and eight), was to take a humorous twist when they pointed out that most people in the village were called Morrison (the dominant clan in the area) and that Angus was a very common name as well. Basically, there were so many options as to make a search for this particular Angus Morrison unlikely to succeed.

I could get no recollections from the post office at Kinlochbervie as to sighting number nine which was supposedly reported there, but was more successful when visiting the postmistress at the smaller settlement of Oldshoremore. She pointed out that Sandy Gunn's old cottage was opposite, and took me to visit an elderly lady who lived nearby. Over tea and cakes, the elderly lady explained to me that:

- *To the best of her recollections, Sandwood Cottage had never been occupied by an Australian (see Theory Three).*

- *That the key witness, Sandy Gunn, had always been known as a man who would never tell a lie. Slightly confusingly however, she also recollected that it was a mermaid Sandy Gunn had claimed to see, and knew nothing of him seeing a sailor.*

- *That a local writer, R. MacDonald Robertson, had recorded and published all the ghosts and folklore of the area, and had spoken to many of the witnesses first-hand.*

She kindly directed me to a house between Oldshoremore and Sheigra (an even smaller settlement) where MacDonald Robertson used to live. Over more cakes and tea from my hosts, I was able to establish that MacDonald Robertson's book, *Scottish Highland Folktales*, was the original source work for many of the earlier sightings.

Conclusions of the investigation

As well as the visit to the site described above, the source of these conclusions were also assisted by research I made at Glasgow Central Library and enquiries to the paranormal author Peter Underwood. This brought the conclusions that:

- *Sightings one to six were recorded originally by R. Macdonald Robertson. As a local resident getting his information first-hand, these sightings should be taken seriously.*

- *Sightings seven to ten are reports passed on to the ghost hunter Peter Underwood. Whilst I do not have the same amount of detail as to how this testimony was obtained (first-hand, second-hand, etc.), there are no grounds to think of these as being anything other than accurate reports of claimed sightings.*

- *The idea of the 'ghost' being the 'hermit' James MacRory Smith has an element of appeal. However, his twenty year stay in the area means that he could only have influenced sightings seven to ten. As sightings eight and ten do not really involve a 'bearded sailor', it seems unlikely they involved MacRory Smith so he can in no way be seen as a full explanation for the phenomena.*

- *No evidence was found to in any way connect this ghost story with an Australian despite this theory being repeated in ghost books.*

- *The problems I had with my tape and camera was 'interesting' (there is a theory of malfunction of equipment indicating the presence of ghosts). In hindsight however, and without any other phenomena that night, I would expect this was coincidental.*

- *I concluded that Sandwood was indeed an interesting haunting, with a series of well-documented sightings at regular intervals, by different people over the last half-century. Whilst there may be natural explanations for some of the sightings, the majority remain genuine anomalies.*

As you can see from the above report, whilst nothing had been definitely proved or disproved by using the techniques I suggested earlier in the chapter, a certain amount of sense was made of a series of events which took place over the best part of half a century. In addition, this process of research was a most rewarding experience both in its discovery and in getting the chance to meet and talk to a series of unique and interesting people.

A few years ago I was invited to appear on a Grampian Television programme on the paranormal that was concentrating on the Sandwood Bay haunting. The television company showed me some literature they had gained while researching themselves. This included a report from the Ghost Club Society (the organisation formed after the Ghost Club split in the 1990s) who had also more recently investigated the case.

I was first rather taken aback by a section in the report that seemed to possibly cast doubt on my visit, the argument being that I could not have tackled the walk before dark setting out at 7-7.30 p.m. in April. They had noticed my claim that the walk was two miles whilst they had experienced a four mile walk, not realising that whilst the entire track is now closed off to cars, when I made my visit the first two miles was accessible to motor vehicles. After my initial slight annoyance, I then thought with the information they had, their report made a very fair point indeed.

After all, perhaps the only true rule of researching the paranormal is believe nothing and check and question everything!

nine

SHOULD GHOST HUNTING BE FUN?

Or should we all wear 'hair shirts' when we investigate?

In 2008 I went to a talk by a paranormal investigator with expertise in equipment to listen to his comments on using equipment in ghost hunts. I thought it might add something to the debate that we had in Chapters Five and Six. He very much came from the 'strictly scientific' school of investigation, frowning on such things as séances and Ouija boards. During one part of the talk I looked over to my ghost hunting colleague Rosemary Murdie with a look of disbelief. He had been talking about setting up cameras for remote viewing of a site, but had added how lucky the people watching the cameras would be as they need not even venture out from their base during an investigation! Ghost hunting without exploring a haunted house – we both looked at each other as if to say 'you have to be kidding'. Surely this is like buying fish in a fishmongers rather than catching it with a rod at the end of a windy pier. Yes it might be cold, frustrating and even boring, and at times, but to turn the essence of the discipline into simply watching monitors would be to change it completely.

Ghost hunting has what I would call 'Cavaliers' and 'Roundheads'. (By a Cavalier I do not mean the modern implication of being slipshod and unfocused, but rather the original meaning of doing things with a certain colour, style and sense of fun.) Both types of people are genuine seekers of the unknown, but both take on their task in very different ways. This chapter is about the 'Cavalier'-type attitude to ghost hunting that I believe makes it of greater reward to the volunteer, whilst not necessarily taking away its scientific edge. A Cavalier, for example, would spend the night sleeping in a haunted bed (as Harry Price did with Professor Joad). A Roundhead would put sensors between the sheets. A good ghost hunt would use both the sleeper in the bed and the sensors in the bed at different times. The question is, which would you rather be doing?

The difference between these two approaches within a ghost hunt itself has largely been covered in Chapter Six, where I have stated that (with certain provisos) it is legitimate to use scientifically controversial methods of investigation so long as the limitations of these methods are taken into account. Whilst I feel that these techniques are legitimate to any investigation (although others would disagree), they also have the added bonus of making an investigation far more interesting, and closer to the archetypical experience you would expect a ghost hunt to give. This is not a bad thing as we are all volunteers, and an investigation should be something to be relished, not thought of as a chore.

Over and above these alternative investigation techniques there are two main areas in which the ghost hunting experience can be heightened:

- *The way in which you use your findings and expertise outside of an investigation.*

- *Choosing sites which are of particular interest to investigate in their own right.*

Just before Christmas 2008, I went to a meeting of the SPR and heard a very different type of speaker to the equipment expert I mentioned previously. The speaker in question was

Eddie Brazil who, along with Paul Adams and the veteran ghost
hunter Peter Underwood, had been compiling a definitive guide
to the haunting of Borley Rectory. All three speakers made good
contributions that night, but it was particularly Eddie Brazil's
opening remarks that got my attention. He explained that ever
since he had been reading about the paranormal in his teens,
he had imagined what it would have been like giving a talk to
the SPR and imagined how it would have been to work in co-
operation with Peter Underwood, who was then almost certainly
the best-known ghost hunter in the country. (These were not far
from the same ambitions I also had two or three decades ago.) So
in that one night, Eddie Brazil ensured the fulfilment of two of
his major ghost hunting ambitions, without going anywhere near
a haunted house.

I highly suspect that many people involved in the subject for
some time have some kind of similar ambition over and above
simply investigating haunted house after haunted house. They
may wish to be published or appear on television or perhaps just
lecture on their views. All are perfectly respectable ambitions
which can heighten the experience of being a ghost hunter. Some
are surprisingly easy to achieve, so long as you have first done your
investigating thoroughly and have something to say.

I have listed below the main ambitions that I have found some,
or most, ghost hunters wish to achieve, and give brief advice as to
if and how they can be fulfilled.

Featuring your ghost hunting activities in the local press
If you belong to an established and competent local investigations
group, it should not be at all difficult to appear in the local press
when investigating a site in the area. This is, of course, assuming
that the owners of the site wish the publicity. If they do not, their
wishes should of course be respected. Local press love to print
off-beat 'human interest' stories. They are especially fond of such
stories that ghost hunters can contribute in the run up period to
Hallowe'en. In addition the publicity may get you more cases, as
well as the satisfaction that what you are doing is newsworthy.

The downside to remember is that your average local reporter knows absolutely nothing about the paranormal and may even try to turn it into a 'fun' story. Reporters on the whole though are not deliberately malicious (though some other ghost hunters may think differently), and two simple steps should tend to overcome this.

Firstly, remember to carefully explain what ghost hunters are, as many people, including reporters, still picture men with backpacks as per the 1984 *Ghostbusters* movie. This should minimise the chances of a spoof story.

Secondly, always give the reporter a press release (i.e. a written summary of your investigations). Such press releases can sometimes almost be reproduced in the story if well written (saving the reporter time rewriting it), and can ensure your report and conclusions come over far more accurately than via a telephone or face-to-face interview.

With this strategy you would be unfortunate to get a story that you are very unhappy with. However, what you will never get control of is the headline. If you investigate a haunted pub, the headline may be a bad pun such as 'Spirits served up after hours in local pub'. I made that one up myself, but it gives a fairly good idea of what to expect.

Putting ghost hunting activities into the national press

If you have a normal investigation with one or two unexplained creaks or bangs and a fleeting glimpse of something from the corner of your eye, do not even think of approaching the national press – they will not be interested. The national press will only feature stories which have a particular angle over and above the haunting. A family being genuinely terrorised by an evil spirit would perhaps be successful, but then again a terrorised family would not normally seek to be in the national press. The Enfield Poltergeist, which did get national press coverage, achieved this because the family in question actually initially called the *Daily Mirror* asking for help. If the help, in the form of the investigators Maurice Grosse and Guy Playfair, had arrived prior to the newspaper finding out, it is unlikely the case would have achieved the same amount of coverage.

The 'twist' in the tale required can sometimes have nothing to do with the actual haunting itself. For example, a few years ago a minor haunting was widely reported in the national newspapers simply because the new owners of a house were considering suing the former owners because they withheld the fact that it was haunted in their sales pack. One of the few times I have witnessed national press interest was when myself and other members of the Ghost Club were participating in the 'World Dracula Congress' in Transylvania. This included an eclectic mix of speakers on Dracula, folklore, and the paranormal. Whilst not in any way an investigation, it did include the wonderfully exotic 'art experiment' by the artist Roman Vasseur, who exported a box of soil from near Dracula's castle to the UK, leaving people with the idea that it may turn into a vampire on arriving at its destination. (This would have replicated what happened in the *Dracula* novel by Bram Stoker).

As a paranormal experiment (if that was ever what it was) it was never going to succeed, but as a wonderful bit of artistic whimsy it was undoubtedly worth him doing, and as a ghost hunter I was perfectly happy to be part of a conference that promoted it. Ghost hunters after all should not always take themselves too seriously.

That said, unless you know of a terrorised family who actually want publicity, a very unorthodox congress approaching, or some such equivalent twist, you will probably be wasting your time approaching the national press. There are, after all, far more reliable methods of putting your message across.

Putting your ghost hunting activities on local television and radio
This is far easier than obtaining national press coverage because local television and radio are always on the lookout for quirky 'human interest' stories in the region that they cover.

The Ghost Club, for example, had some regional television coverage for its series of investigations in Ham House appearing on

'London Tonight' in a Hallowe'en feature. The club also got coverage for simply conducting a talk about the famous 'Hammersmith ghost' on the anniversary of a ghost hunter shooting a man who he thought was the ghost. This emphasises the media's desire for a 'twist in the tale' to report, for the meeting was not only the 200th anniversary, but it took place in the Black Lion Pub where the inquest had originally been held after the shooting. As with newspapers, any initial contact with television or radio should be made in the form of a well-written press release explaining why the story is newsworthy.

Putting your ghost hunting activities on national television and radio

The first thing to do is to forget about making any direct approaches to national television. National television companies work to their own schedules which are unlikely to be changed by a press release or phone call from a ghost hunting society.

If you have an extremely strong idea for television that you wish to convey, the way to do it is to approach the large number of independent production companies that now exist, who may in turn lobby one of the channels to finance the programme. A list of these production companies can be found in the PACT (i.e. the Producers Alliance for Cinema and Television), full details of which can been found by an internet search.

Even approaching production companies is very much a long shot. However, that does not necessarily mean that your chance to put your views across on national television will never occur. If you are part of a well-established organisation with (very importantly) a good website, there is always a chance you will be approached or emailed by a television researcher when they are making a programme which could be relevant to your experiences.

Such contacts need not necessarily stop at national boundaries. For example, I have been contacted in the past by Japanese film crews who were making documentaries about English ghosts.

These have led on two occasions to subsequent documentary film shoots.

Giving talks and participating in debates

Of course. ensuring that your findings are circulated does not necessarily mean publicising them in the media. There is also a small paranormal speakers' circuit in which you could hopefully be given a chance to explain your work.

Regular monthly speakers have always been organised by both the Ghost Club and the SPR, and I am sure both organisations would consider favourably an approach from a researcher with something interesting to say. The SPR also has a more academically focused annual conference which welcomes applications from potential speakers outside of the organisation. It is also worth emphasising that for this and other events you do not have to be a presenter to get something out of it, as much of the debate comes from questioning the speakers and swapping ideas late into the night.

Other forums for either speaking or participating in include:

- *The several 'Skeptics in the Pub' groups which exist around the country.*

- *Occasional conferences organised by Parasearch, sometimes in association with other organisations.*

- *The 'Unconvention' organised by the* Fortean Times *and normally held in London. (This is by far the largest-scale conference on the paranormal).*

- *For those who want something slightly more exotic, the Transylvanian Society of Dracula (TSD) in Romania sometimes hold conferences with a slightly more paranormal twist, as opposed to those with a purely 'Dracula' theme.*

Participating in ghost tourism

It is not uncommon for a local ghost hunter to also carry out ghost walks in their areas. It is sometimes also the case that ghost hunters may give guided tours and ghost hunting tasters at haunted sites. So long as these fee-earning activities are kept very separate from their more serious investigations, I see this as a harmless extension of their activities.

Publishing your findings

By far the easiest way to do this of course via a website, especially if you or the organisation you belong to has one. Many excellent paranormal websites have sprung up over the last decade which are very professionally constructed and fairly well read. However you may wish to go one stage further than self-publication on the net, but unfortunately there are few commercial magazines which delve into the paranormal.

Of those that do exist, by far the best known is the *Fortean Times*. This has a far wider remit than just the areas of the paranormal normally investigated by ghost hunters, covering such things as strange deaths, UFOs etc. It normally has around three guest writers a month, so by definition competition is fierce. Less readily available in the newsagents is the well presented *Paranormal* magazine. Here, if you present the editor with a good article it is likely to be published.

What remains is what is perhaps the holy grail of publishing achievements to a ghost hunter (or, indeed, anyone else particularly passionate about a particular interest), which is of course the publication of a book on the subject. The first and most important thing required here is a good idea, a good bit of research and hopefully a way of making it a little bit unique. Over and above that, it is worth noting that the ghost book market has changed a lot over the past two decades. It primarily consists now of:

🖎 *Spin-off books from television series'. Especially at the time of writing, books written by various persons who have featured in* Most Haunted.

❧   *Books about ghosts in a particular region or town. The History Press
     do a wide selection of these.*

❧   *Books about one particularly intense haunting.* The South Shields
     Poltergeist *is one of most recent.*

❧   *Glossy gazetteers, of which the author Richard Jones has written a
     good selection.*

❧   *The occasional book which does not fit into any of these categories.*

Unless you are a television star or an established author, it is most
unlikely you would be commissioned to write a television spin-
off or a glossy gazetteer. If you have a particularly intense ongoing
case, or have thought up a unique angle on a book that does not
fit into any category, then there is certainly some potential for a
publication. However, by far the easiest way to start is to write a
book on ghosts in your region or town. If you are a member of
the leading investigations group in your area, you are probably the
leading authority on your area's ghosts. This type of book often
gets into tourist shops under the guise of a guidebook, rather than
just in the paranormal section of book stores big enough to have
such a section.

It is also worth noting that due to many small publishers being
taken over, there are few publishers that are both interested in the
paranormal and willing to take on authors without agents. In turn,
there are few agents that have any real desire to take on unpub-
lished paranormal writers. You may find therefore that there are
only seven or eight publishers who are both accessible and willing
to take this type of book seriously. The rule of thumb is generally
that if a publisher is not already publishing books on the paranormal, that publisher is unlikely to suddenly want to start. A look at
the publishers of paranormal books already on the shelves of book
stores will therefore give a very good idea of who to approach.
Anyone who is even thinking of trying to publish should obtain
a copy of *The Writers and Artists Yearbook*, which gives far better

insight on how to approach things than I could possibly do in this short section of this book.

With all the above ways of bringing your thoughts to an audience, there is one question which I have so far avoided but which most people deep down really want to know. Can a ghost hunter make a living, or at least make some money, from their non-investigative endeavours?

Whilst very few will make a living from ghost hunting, as a matter of principal I have always thought it correct that if a television company is paying the producer, the cameraman etc. they should pay for the interviewee (unless he or she has specifically requested the interview). There is also a certain thrill of being paid (and thus being valued) for doing something that you really like doing, which goes beyond any monetary value itself. It is always quite possible that you may not even appear on a show when agreed. This happened to some colleagues and I who were asked to appear on an edition of the *Barrymore* show as paranormal experts in the audience. The show, however, was running very late in a stiflingly hot theatre and our particular section was dropped. Just as well then that we had requested some kind of fee.

I have normally found the reaction of most television companies is to rarely offer a fee initially but often to do so when asked. An enthusiastic programme researcher may ring you telling you how much fun it would be. At this stage, politely pointing out that everyone else in the studio is being paid for 'having fun' normally does the trick. If, however, it is a subject that you are very keen to give your views on it is worth bearing in mind that such an approach does not always work.

Having pointed out the slight reluctance to pay ghost hunters normal appearance fees, it is also worth pointing out that on the day they usually treat ghost hunters with respect, and the enthusiastic researcher who says it will be fun is normally right. For me, there was, for example, nothing quite likes the experience of being flown up to Scotland to be interviewed for a forthcoming television show about the ghost of Sandwood Bay. If you get such a chance to give insight into your favourite haunted site, be sure to take it.

Below is a summary of the likelihood of some payment for your activities related to ghost hunts:

- *Inclusion in the press – very little chance at all.*

- *Radio – some kind of fee is normally paid if brought into the studio. This is less likely if they interview you at home or at a haunted site.*

- *Television – something close to the average hourly wage is often achievable.*

- *Magazines – the* Fortean Times *pays a reasonable writer's fee.*

- *Speakers fees, or at the very least travelling expenses, are often paid by paranormal organisations who tend of course to value your work as peers.*

- *Should you get to the book publication stage, you should expect to be treated like any other author.*

To summarise this chapter so far; ghost hunting is a newsworthy and popular activity. There is nothing wrong with enjoying this fact by making your serious contributions public, and in some cases charging the media for your time. In contrast, there is everything wrong with charging an anxious house owner for investigating their ghost – this should never be done. It will leave you open to accusations of exploitation, and in some cases those accusations may even be correct!

If the first part of this chapter was about enjoying the publicity that the pursuit of a unique interest can bring, the second part is very much about ensuring that the actual ghost hunt is an enjoyable experience.

Some practical suggestions with regards to the type of sites to avoid, and the right balance of people to create a relaxed and constructive vigil, have already been offered in Chapter Six. This chapter will go a little further, however, in suggesting specific places, and types of places, that can either be investigated, or at the very least visited to soak up the unique atmosphere.

So what makes the perfect haunted location? It must surely feature several of the following elements:

- *Remoteness – the feeling that it would be difficult to leave before dawn.*

- *History – premises that are famous for something, even if only locally.*

- *Recent reported activity – self-evidently true as that is what a ghost hunt is really about.*

- *A haunted reputation – the type of place that makes villagers turn and stare in the local pub when you announce your intentions to stay.*

- *An atmospheric place to stay – by this I of course mean 'scary'.*

- *The owners should believe in the ghost – there is nothing worse than getting to a location and being told that the owner thinks the stories of the haunting are just superstition.*

If a location has several of these factors it is unlikely the night will be dull; if it has most or all of these factors, the night could be extremely intense and exhilarating.

Unfortunately some sites, such as Borley Church or the site of the former rectory, whilst ticking nearly all of these boxes fail one most essential test. Namely, that it is difficult or impossible to stay in these locations for the purpose of an investigation. In the case of the site of Borley Rectory, this is simply because there have been several properties built over it. I often wonder why a well-off ghost hunter (if there is such a thing) didn't take the opportunity to buy the plot at the time. As things stand, however, the resident's privacy should of course be respected.

In the case of Borley Church, its exclusion from investigations is simply because of the nuisance caused by excessive ghost tourists. This has angered some of the villagers and led them to keep the church locked. Borley is for now an example of a wonderfully interesting investigation site which cannot be investigated any more. There are many more of these which are frustrating for any ghost hunter. Fortunately there are still many which remain happy to allow investigations; some even make a small business these days out of doing so. Other sites, such as ruins and the open country-side, can be freely accessible.

There are probably well over 100 accessible haunted sites in the UK which have the potential to send shivers down a ghost hunter's spine. I will suggest some of my favourites below, includ-ing ones I have visited and others that I very much hope to visit in the future. Whilst I am suggesting that it is fine for ghost hunters to enjoy the thrill of ghost hunting by visiting sites with an 'edge', they should not do so in an irresponsible way, and any required permissions should always be sought.

The Ram Inn, Wotton-under-Edge, Gloucestershire

If you expect to have a quiet pint at the Ram Inn prior to taking on a long night's ghost hunting, you will be in for quite a long wait. The inn has not had a license since 1968. Shortly afterwards it was purchased by John Humphries, a colourful and friendly character who still owns it to this day.

Parts of the Ram date back to the twelfth century and John has made it his labour of love to gradually restore it ever since. He also quickly became aware of many strange happenings and several ghosts were identified, including a phantom cavalier, a witch, a monk and a mysterious black cat. There are three things that make the Ram Inn a particularly special experience for ghost hunters:

Firstly, as a private dwelling it has not been subject to any of the modernisations you would expect in a working pub. It has all the authentic flavour of a truly ancient building.

Secondly, it has a reputation for having a malevolent atmos-phere. This basically means that whilst nothing physically bad has happened to any of their guests, it has the potential to be a truly frightening place. Any ghost hunter who deep down does not consider this a plus is in the wrong hobby.

Finally, since his paranormal experiences, John has become very accommodating to ghost hunters, and in the past has been amenable to overnight stays by arrangement. I have had the pleasure of spending a night at the Ram some time ago, and whilst nothing significant happened that night, I can assure you it is a unique and intriguing site.

Charlton House, Charlton, South-East London

A seventeenth-century Jacobean mansion, Charlton House brings both the atmosphere of an old stately home, and the convenience of easy accessibility for London-based ghost hunters.

The outside of the house is very imposing, giving the appearance of a typical haunted house. These days, however, the interior is a little less authentic as it is partly used as a conference and community centre and the Jacobean furniture has now long been replaced by rows of identical chairs. Charlton House continues to be blessed with two spine-tingling ghost stories, and a high level of activity.

The principle haunting surrounds a previous owner of the house, Sir Wiliam Langhorne, who purchased it in 1680. Sir William is infamous for marrying a seventeen-year-old bride a few months before his death in 1715. After living life to the full, his ghost has continued in a similar way and is meant to continue paying particular attention to the ladies. The second, particularly 'attractive', ghost story surrounds a servant girl seen wandering through the grounds with a baby in her arms. Though her identity is unknown, mummified remains of a baby were actually discovered in a chimney during renovations after a bomb attack during the Second World War.

There appears to be quite a high level of poltergeist-type activity that happens in the house, with tales of crockery being thrown and smashed as well as our own investigation which produced the flying wooden mushroom. There are also many other types of phenomena such as the sound of sighing and the sensation of being pushed. The house has also produced some more interesting than average orb photographs, which I have explained more about in the section on orbs in Chapter Five.

Charlton House is owned by Greenwich Council, who have in the past been fairly amenable to allowing part and whole-night investigations.

The Hellfire Caves and the George and Dragon Inn, West Wycombe, Buckinghamshire

This site was one of the first I read about when a teenager with a thirst for the paranormal. I naively even tried to organise a 'ghost hunt' there at the tender age of fourteen with some school friends. This was abandoned when, not surprisingly, all my friends were banned by their parents from going (which was just as well as the pub I had identified was actually the George and Dragon, West Wickham, in Kent). To this date I have not yet made up for my teenage error and investigated these sites properly. I have, however, visited both and can assure you they would make for an excellent investigation.

In contrast with the modern metropolis of High Wycombe, West Wycombe – a village of basically one main street – appears to be in a time capsule. In some ways it is, as the whole village is actually owned and preserved by the National Trust.

The caves themselves are not a natural phenomenon, but were created as something of a folly in the 1750s by the philanderer Francis Dashwood. Strangely, although Dashwood had a reputation for being a man of amoral tendencies, and primarily used the caves for the excesses of his infamous Hellfire Club, the original reason for building them was to provide employment for local farmers following a series of harvest failures.

The caves are clearly manmade with wonderful Gothic arches, rooms and alcoves. They combine a sense of enchantment, with a claustrophobic and eerie atmosphere. There is even rumoured to be a tunnel between the caves and the George and Dragon, although that has never been found.

The caves are reputed to be haunted by Hellfire Club member and poet Sir Paul Whitehead, but the most famous ghost of the caves and the pub is known as 'Sukie'. She was apparently a barmaid from the George and Dragon who had a lover above her status, who she thought she was to marry in a secret ceremony in the caves. This turned out to be a practical joke laid on by three of Sukie's former suitors from the village. In the argument that ensued, Sukie hit her head on the floor and died. The suitors apparently 'covered their tracks' by returning her body back to her room in the inn.

This is a story that is crying out for further research, as like the tale of the *Lady Lovibond*, who would have communicated such detailed facts? Sukie was dead, and her former suitors would not have passed on the story and sent themselves to the gallows. Despite this weakness in this particular story, both the George and Dragon and the caves are wonderfully atmospheric places to visit. The George and Dragon has accommodation so can be used as a place to stay after a late night investigation in the caves. The caves are open for hire and so are accessible to investigate with the right approach. I would highly recommend these sites.

Ham House, Richmond, Surrey

The full details of this haunting are discussed in Chapter Eight. However, it is also worth adding that the house's atmospheric nature, when combined with the colourful tales of murder relating to the ghost, makes this an interesting and indeed spooky place to visit. The curators of the premises did allow a series of well-organised investigations to take place a few years ago. Whilst it is currently unclear as to their attitude towards further projects, it is also worth noting that they organise occasional 'ghost tours' of the premises themselves.

This is a site well worthy of a daytime visit, even if an overnight stay proves impossible.

Clerkenwell House of Detention, Clerkenwell, London

This is another wonderfully atmospheric underground site which consists of the intact basement of a demolished Victorian prison. In its time the House of Detention was London's busiest remand centre, catering for over 10,000 prisoners a year. After the disused premises reopened as a museum in the early 1990s, unusual occurrences were reported, including the sobs of a little girl and strange footsteps. It made an excellent place to investigate in central London being historic, creepy and totally removed from the noise of the bustling city above. The Ghost Club held several interesting investigations there during this period.

My last encounter with the House of Detention, however, was scrambling in via the fire exit for a television documentary on haunted London in the year 2000. The site had been repossessed from the museum management only the day before and whilst, after hurried renegotiations, filming went ahead, the main entrance remained barred. Trying to find a way into a prison rather than find a way out was a most surreal experience.

The lease on the prison was subsequently passed onto another party and access for investigation purposes became far more difficult. I am unaware as to the exact situation when writing this book, and this would be a challenge of research and negotiation skills just to organise an investigation. It would however be a most rewarding challenge if successful.

The Ferry Boat Inn, Holywell, Cambridgeshire

The Ferry Boat Inn makes claims to be the oldest inn in England and that alcoholic beverages were sold there as far back as AD 560. It is a wonderful thatched building on the banks of the Great Ouse which, as well as being a pub, offers overnight accommodation.

The inn has long been famous for the ghost of a 'white lady' and séances conducted by SPR members in the second half of the twentieth century put 'flesh to the bones' of this apparition. The séances named the ghost as being the tragic figure of Juliet Tewsley, a local girl who lived in the eleventh century. At the tender age of seventeen, Juliet fell in love with a woodcutter's son. On being rejected she committed suicide on 17 March 1050 and as suicides could not be buried in consecrated ground, her remains were buried near the inn. The inn was later extended to cover her grave, and there is indeed a flagstone which is a different shape to the rest. This is supposed to mark the spot where Juliet was buried.

Although information picked up by séances is not always accurate, giving the ghost a name and a tragic tale has greatly heightened interest. The ghost is supposed to always appear on the anniversary of her death, and it has been known for up to 400 people to come to the pub to witness this. There is little chance then of a conventional ghost hunt on the ghost's anniversary, but every chance of witnessing a unique celebration of the paranormal.

Colleagues of mine from the ghost club, for example, witnessed a recital of poetry inspired by the ghost when they visited it a few years ago, and met other paranormal researchers interested in this tale.

The anniversary is a unique event for ghost hunters who wish just for one evening to shed themselves of their equipment and just enjoy taking in the atmosphere and the folklore (and, of course, the possibility that it may all be true).

Chingle Hall, Goosenargh, Lancashire

For much of the 1980s and '90s, Chingle Hall was regarded as the most haunted house in England. This status was heightened when a particularly scary feature appeared on the very popular *Strange but True* television series.

During that period, Chingle Hall undoubtedly took advantage of its reputation by organising (and charging for) numerous overnight stays, both for ghost hunters and thrill seekers. These stays did however produce a good range of phenomena.

Chingle Hall was built in 1260 by a knight named Singleton and is considered to be one of the oldest moated manor houses still in existence. It is most famous though as the birthplace of John Wall, who was born there in 1620 and who was later canonised by the Catholic Church after being hung, drawn and quartered for his missionary work in a staunchly Protestant England. It is possible that the monk who is frequently seen at the hall is the ghost of John Wall. The other 'identifiable' ghost is that of Eleanor Singleton who was reputedly kept captive in a room at the hall for a period of twelve years until her death, aged twenty. Related phenomena have included the smell of lavender and tug of people's clothing.

Chingle is included in this list predominately because the amount of positive testimony in itself would make it a most interesting place to stay. However, I must admit my own stay at Chingle, while well worth it for the above reason, was otherwise a little disappointing. The hall, though steeped in history, is actually a relatively small building, and more importantly nothing of note happened there that evening.

It is much more difficult to visit Chingle Hall these days, but should the opportunity arise it would still certainly be worth trying to stay in the place that held a popular claim as England's most haunted house for many years.

Woodchester Mansion, Nympsfield, Gloucestershire

I have mentioned various ghost hunting experiences at Woodchester Mansion in this book so far. What I have not fully described is the unbelievable uniqueness of this site. The mansion is an inspiring example of over-the-top Gothic revivalism and yet it comes without glass in the main windows or any signs of the necessities of comfortable living within. This is not because the mansion has been left to decay, it is rather because it was never completed in the first place. It is a Victorian masterpiece in the making, which has been waiting for well over 100 years for the builders to return from their tea break.

Woodchester Mansion was conceived by William Leigh, who bought the estate for £100,000 in the mid-nineteenth century and wished to replace the existing house with something more impressive. With the help of the brilliant young architect Benjamin Bucknall, the main exterior was completed and roofed by 1866. However when Leigh died in 1873, shortages of funds meant that the project was put permanently on ice, except for a completed apartment within the building that his descendants continued to live in. Today it has the strange distinction of being perhaps the only listed building that was never actually fully built.

As the mansion was never formally occupied it is difficult to actually speculate as to who or what any of the ghosts actually are. Nevertheless there has been a fairly impressive range of phenomena, from a lady being seen at a window under which a floor was never built, to phantom horsemen in the driveway, and a floating head in the bathroom.

The Woodchester Mansion Trust has allowed ghost hunts to take place on several occasions and talks of the results on its own web page. There is therefore every opportunity that responsible investigators could take further advantage of this wonderful site – ideal for a 'warm weather' investigation. To ensure some comfort before returning home, the Rose and Crown at nearby Nympsfield also provides a limited amount of accommodation.

The White Lady of Coalisland, County Tyrone, Northern Ireland

With the above examples of exceptionally interesting places to investigate, there often seems to be an event or catalyst which turns a haunting from a 'run of the mill' affair to a must see attraction for ghost hunters. It is quite possible that even as this book is being written, an up-till-now anonymous site is suddenly, (either through increased activity or increased publicity) becoming the latest essential place to investigate.

Coalisland is a small former mining town of some 6,000 people which has occasional sightings of a female phantom hitchhiker on the nearby Mullaghmoyle Road. Yet towards the end of 2008, sightings became focused around a burnt-out, ruined old house on the road which, due to its condition, has rightfully been described as a ghost hunter's paradise. The number of ghostly sightings also increased exponentially, with one local resident alone claiming to have seen the ghost twenty times. The 'old ruined house' location of the sightings has captured the imagination both of ghost hunters and ghost tourists in the area with the result that on some nights up to sixty cars can be parked near the premises. The identity of the ghost has not yet been established to date, but some locals have speculated it is not a 'normal' ghost. Rather it may be an escaped 'bottled spirit'. There had been a tradition in Ireland in past times to trap an exorcised spirit in a bottle under a tree, and there had been tree-felling nearby where one such spirit was supposed to be trapped. This is a fascinating piece of Irish folklore and a hypothesis which needs to be tested like any other.

Press interest came first in the form of the local paper, the *Tyrone Gazette*. The story was then run by the *Belfast Times* and subsequently by three of the main national British newspapers. It is, at the time of writing, far too early to tell just how much substance or longevity this haunting has. When the initial frenzy has died down a little it would be a fascinating task for investigators to discover both the substance of the claims and the history of the house. It is worth after all remembering that even Borley Rectory was only a locally known haunted site before the *Daily Mirror* ran articles on it and turned it into a national phenomenon. Coalisland is a very well witnessed case that may well also be long lasting.

Poenari Castle, Wallachia, Romania

There is a certain amount of debate as to whether this site is actually haunted or not. Based on its history it certainly should be and even the possibility that it might be makes this site worthy of investigation. The castle was built by the Romanian tyrant Vlad Dracula (also known as Vlad the Impaler, and the character from which Bram Stoker created the novel *Dracula*). However, Bram Stoker never visited Romania and his geographical understanding of the region was quite limited. Vlad Dracula was actually a prince in the region of Walachia, not Transylvania where his novel was based, and the story of Dracula should quite clearly have been based around the high cliffs of Poenari in Walachia. Even forgetting about fictional vampire novels, Poenari has quite a history which would make a haunting likely.

Vlad Dracula was prince of the small state of Walachia in the mid-fifteenth century. He rebuilt the fortress with the slave labour of his enemies and used it as an impregnable base against the constantly invading Turkish forces. Vlad's tactics in this campaign were basically akin to a mixture of terrorism and psychological warfare, which was perhaps necessary considering his troops were continually outnumbered. His nickname of 'the Impaler' largely came from his tactic of impaling prisoners and enemies on stakes, sometimes in the hope of demoralising the oncoming Turkish army when they saw what may await them.

Whilst this tactic had a large element of success, Vlad was eventually defeated at his Poenari stronghold, where it is said his wife threw herself from the battlements to avoid being caught. Although Vlad initially escaped, he was eventually captured and (almost certainly) killed by the Turks. His body though was never found.

The confusing thing about Poenari is that due to the association with the fictional vampire story of Bram Stoker, it has increasingly become a centre for vampire hunters rather than ghost hunters. According to Romanian folklore, however, Vlad Dracula is said to still haunt the place.

Getting to the truth of such a claim in a foreign country can be particularly tricky. It has been claimed that at least one descendant of Dracula's enemies has died suddenly when visiting the castle in the 1930s, and certainly there are more recent claims of strange experiences at the fortress. It was also investigated by the popular American television series *Ghost Hunters International*. Whilst this is not the best recorded ghost story by any means, it is the absolute essence of ghost hunting as an 'interest'. The forbidding hill fortress has to be seen to truly be appreciated, and the views after a 1,400 step climb are by themselves near to being supernatural.

Unfortunately (or perhaps fortunately) my visit was only made during daylight hours so I cannot vouch for what would happen after dark. Even if the spirit of Vlad is long gone, it is quite possible you may believe differently after a night in this awe-inspiring place.

Pluckley, Kent

A wonderfully quaint settlement in the heart of Kent, Pluckley has for a long while had a reputation for being England's most haunted village. This reputation though is gained through the number of ghosts rather than the level of their activity.

Nevertheless, Pluckley has become a must visit both for serious ghost hunters and ghost tourists, and this quiet village has been known to have a police presence at Hallowe'en to control the crowds.

Perhaps the fascination of the place is that Pluckley seems to have nearly every type of archetypical ghost. Some of the main ones have been identified as:

- *A highwayman at the aptly named Fright Corner.*

- *The sound of a phantom coach on Maltmans Hill.*

- *A gypsy woman seen on Pinnock Bridge.*

- *A suicidal schoolmaster on Dicky Buss's Lane.*

- *Ghostly ladies abound; a red lady haunts the grounds of St Nicolas' Church, while a white lady and a Tudor lady haunt two local houses.*

- *The grounds of a house called Greystones are reputedly haunted by a monk.*

- *All three pubs in the area have their ghostly tales as well. The Black Horse has suffered from some poltergeist activity. If you go to the Derring Arms for its delicious food, you may also encounter an old lady in a bonnet, while the Blacksmiths Arms is haunted by a Cavalier.*

The locations of all these sites in the village and on its outskirts actually makes for an excellent two or three-mile ghost walk. This is made better still by the fact that many of these sites are either publicly accessible outdoor sites, or in publicly accessible buildings such as pubs and churches. The publicly accessible outdoor areas make it tempting to organise an impromptu ghost hunt as many groups have done before. Care should be taken however not to disturb the locals if considering such a project.

To date, other than at Hallowe'en, I have not heard of too many complaints of excessive ghost hunting from villagers, and I am sure that the pubs enjoy the additional trade that it brings. Every attempt should be made to keep it that way, to avoid this becoming a site like Borley where ghost hunters can be treated with suspicion and disdain.

Surprisingly for such a famously haunted village, I am not aware of any mention of it amongst the late nineteenth and early twentieth-century ghost authors such as Charles Harper and T.H. Thiselton-Dyer. The first mention I am aware of is as late as 1955 in the book *Pluckley Was My Playground* by Frederick Saunders. This only mentioned some of the ghosts, and a local man has apparently claimed that during the 1950s he invented some additional tales for journalists.

Alternatively though, Pluckley's omission from historic ghost books can also be explained by the fact that most of the earlier ghost writers concentrated on major places and important buildings. Pluckley could simply have been too rural for them to discover its legends.

Incidentally, like Poenari Castle, Pluckley also appeared on the *Ghost Hunters International* television show, and my impression is that their policy is to select and visit some of the most interesting and unique haunted locations on the planet. I wonder if they have any vacancies in their team!

Sandwood Bay and the north-east tip of Sutherland, Scotland
Much has already been said in this book about the haunting at Sandwood Bay, and for full details of this I will refer you back to Chapter Eight. This final example of a truly interesting place to ghost hunt is more to describe the other haunts that surround Sandwood and the unique wilderness atmosphere that is not found in quite the same way anywhere else in Britain. Mark Alexander, in his book *Enchanted Britain* (1981), talks about geographical areas where there is a 'thin veil' between the natural and the supernatural. He says that:

> There are certain natural spots which have an enduring mystic qual-
> ity… Sometimes this quality has inspired legends which have become
> associated with them, yet one only has to visit them to realise it is not
> legends which have given rise to their supernormal reputation.

Mark Alexander goes on to identify the area around Sandwood Bay as being one such place where the veil is thin. Leaving Ullapool and heading northwards to Sandwood Bay, it is quite true that the whole area takes on a very special enchanted feeling. Despite there not being a settlement of any size, the whole area is steeped in myths and legends. You drive past ruins as if they were part of the natural scenery, left lying there in a desolate wilderness to decay.

Such places include Ardvreck Castle, once the home of the Macleod clan. This is haunted by a tall grey man and the daughter of one of the Macleod chieftains. Shortly after come the more modern ruins modern of Calda House, former home of the Mackenzies, which burnt down and was never rebuilt after their defeat at the Battle of Culloden. Calda House is haunted by a ghostly lady and by mysterious lights.

Sanctuary from the wilderness may be sought at the pictur-esque Kylesku Hotel until you find this too is possibly haunted by a ghost called Todeas, a local fisherman accidentally killed by his son who pushed him though a trap door down into the 'Snuggery' bar. You will still hear tales of mermaids from some older folk in the area, while the only village of any size, Scourie, was known in past times for its 'storm witch' (a witch who can change the weather to the detriment of ships).

It seems to some that make this drive that there are more ghosts and legends than people to be seen. Your car trundles along a long, winding road surrounded by low mountains of strange shapes, and you remember stories of unseen hands taking control of car wheels on this road. It is at times like this a ghost hunter realises that there is so much more to his interest than ultrasound detec-tors and EMF metres. There is also a mysterious passion for the folklore, the unexplained and the spine-tingling mystery of it all.

Whatever equipment or science is used in the future, such experiences should never be taken away.

If (as Mark Alexander suggested) the veil between the normal and the paranormal is thin in certain areas, this lifting of the veil should not just be measured – it should also be 'experienced'. That is what the 'Cavalier' style of ghost hunter sets out to achieve.

ten

CONCLUSIONS

A new science or just a waste of time?

Chapter One of this book started by pointing out that Pliny the Younger recorded a ghost hunt as early as AD 100. Two millennia later we are still hunting these illusive creatures. Surely this must be the longest-running game of hide and seek in history? Although very many people claim to experience ghosts in some form or another, even after 2,000 years objective evidence remains sparse and often ambiguous. Do sceptics not have every right then to question whether there is anything paranormal to find? This though would be a convenient parody of the situation as the search for ghosts has been hindered by:

- 1,700 years of religious intolerance of the proper investigation of the subject. (This hindrance continued till the late eighteenth century and was fully discussed in Chapter One).

- An inability to fit ghosts even tentatively into Newtonian physics.

If the mainstream science of the day is not able to even comprehend concepts beyond mechanical causes and effects, ghosts and other aspects of the paranormal simply could not have been scientifically discovered. Paranormal phenomena fit far more comfortably within the early twentieth-century theories of Einstein and his successors. It is only since this door opened that true scientific investigation has become possible.

Until fairly recently investigators merely tried to record rather than to explain the paranormal. I subtitled Chapter Four 'You ca not hunt what you do not know', yet that is exactly what many of the pioneering ghost hunters tried to do. Much of early ghost hunting was (and to some extent still is) simply about trying to capture phenomena, without much effort being made to explain what that phenomenon was. This was partly due to an assumption that ghosts (assuming they exist) must be spirits of the dead, an assumption which has only fairly recently been challenged.

Despite 2,000 years of wanting to discover ghosts, real ghost hunting is actually a very new interest. The major alternatives to the survival theory have only really emerged in the second half of the twentieth century, and there is a case for saying that progress has actually been fairly brisk.

One of the major thinkers in this quest to find a workable theory of the supernatural has undoubtedly been the author Colin Wilson. Chapter One of his bestselling book *The Occult* (1979) is actually called 'Magic – The Science of the Future'. In it he postulates that the facility to tune into paranormal activity may be latent in all of us and that evolution has dulled these skills as they are no longer useful for survival.

Nevertheless there is, according to Wilson, the possibility of the return of these abilities at a time of danger or heightened experience. Wilson termed these latent abilities 'Faculty X'. As he explains, 'Faculty X is not a "sixth sense" but an ordinary potentiality of consciousness. And it should be clear... that it is the key not only to the so called occult experience, but to the whole future evolution of the human race' (p. 77).

In some ways this is an incomplete theory in that Wilson does not fully explain what the 'X' in his faculty actually is. In other ways though he importantly points the way to the possibility of making a breakthrough by his suggestion that paranormal powers are still innate within us all and that they can be reawakened under certain moods and conditions. This would certainly explain the emphasis that many put on the correct atmosphere being necessary on any investigation into the paranormal, and why, for example, the art of table tipping takes many sessions to perfect or why it was necessary in the Philip Experiment (see Chapter Six) to create a certain light-hearted atmosphere so as to tap into these powers.

There was actually a period some years ago when I did a certain amount of very uplifting travelling and actually found that a series of unusual coincidences would happen. For example, on several occasions I would be talking about someone who I hadn't seen for some time (in a location such as a bar not connected with them geographically in any way), and that person would suddenly walk in. It would get to the point where part of me started to think I could summon a person up, or more likely part of me was aware that an old friend was nearby.

The one incident that by far outweighed the rest was when I was travelling in Prague alone in 1992, shortly after the fall of the Iron Curtain. I was having difficulty finding accommodation at a reasonable price, and was therefore suitably uplifted when someone handed me a flyer for a new economy hotel in the centre of town. It was clean, modern and secure, being situated next to a very large police station, and I was happy to call it home for the next couple of days. Like all lone travellers I was travelling with a book to read; in my case it was the fascinating *The Book of Laughter and Forgetting* by the renowned Czech author Milan Kundera.

Feeling very pleased with myself for finding my hotel, I spent the first night there relaxing and reading. I came to a chapter of the book that dealt with Kundera's own experiences and how he had been banned from publishing by the former Communist regime. He explained that, 'At the time I had a one room apartment in Prague on Bartolomejska – a short street but a famous one. All the buildings but two (one of which I live in) belong to the Police. Looking down from my large fourth floor window....'

It was at that point I put down the book and a strange shiver went up my spine. I looked at my hotel card and reminded myself that my hotel was indeed situated on Bartolomejska (as Kundera had said, it was indeed a very short street). I looked down from my window, from what was the fourth floor, and could see no other buildings other than the large police station. Remembering that the hotel was new it seemed entirely likely that I was sitting reading of Milan Kundera's experiences on the same spot where had written or at least experienced them himself some twenty years ago. On re-reading the passage of the book (Part 3, The Angels, Section 7), it also seemed that the detailed description of where he lived had little relevance to the rest of the passage. Had my Faculty X somehow guided me to take the flyer and stay in the former house of one of the authors that most inspired me at that time, or had I just got a lucky break when Prague was bulging at the seams that summer? If it was possible then for me to have paranormal experiences as the result of heightened consciousness, it would certainly be possible for anyone. After all, I frequently used to describe myself to colleagues as being as psychic as the average brick, though after thinking more about the 'stone tape' theory this could be rather unfair to the brick.

When Wilson talks of Faculty X, is he talking about the innate ability of a human to actually create the paranormal through phenomena such as ESP or psychokinesis (the ability to move objects with the mind)? Or is this innate power the ability for us to tune in to the paranormal events that are already happening, such as a collective unconsciousness or spirits departed from this life?

Wilson's background at the time of writing *The Occult* was not primarily as a paranormal researcher but more of a researcher and writer on the human psyche. It was perhaps not surprising then that he initially favoured the theory that any paranormal phenomena was caused by the human mind. Following the success of *The Occult* he explored and wrote about the subject further. By the time he wrote the book *Poltergeists* in 1981, he stated that he had changed his mind on the theory that the paranormal were caused purely by latent human energies. Instead he gave serious consideration to the inclusion of a 'mischievous disembodied spirit'. The book included the theory of paranormal researcher Guy Playfair, which Wilson summarised as:

> A football of energy. It somehow gets excluded from disturbed teen-
> agers at puberty. Along come two or three spirits or elementals, look
> through this window and see the football lying around and they
> do what any group of schoolboys would do – they go and kick it
> around… creating havoc.
>
> (pp. 166–67)

This theory, of course, includes both an external spirit and our innate latent power used as a catalyst for the phenomena.

This change of mind appeared to be largely due to his in-depth research on a famous 1960s poltergeist case 'The Black Monk of Pontefract' and his realisation that a non-external agent theory just didn't really fit all of the facts. As Wilson puts it:

> What really changed my mind about the psychokinesis theory is
> was Diane's description of being dragged up the stairs by the entity.
> Nobody in the house on that evening had any doubt as to her terror
> and confusion. It is just conceivable that Diane's unconscious mind
> might throw her out of bed – by way of demanding attention. But
> by no stretch of the imagination can I imagine it grabbing her by the
> throat and dragging her up the stairs.
>
> (p. 169)

Put like that, some kind of spirit theory does in this instance have a plausible ring to it.

While the spirit theories and non-spirit supernatural theories continue to do battle as they have done for the last 100 years, it is only recently that they have been challenged by the 'psycho-logical' theories discussed throughout this book. Namely that a 'paranormal'-type experience can be caused by EMF fields, infra-sound or by just the auto-suggestion of being scared witless in an old, creepy house. The latter of these in particular could help to explain why ghost hunters have a high ratio of unusual expe-riences compared with normal visitors to the same premises. This theory has the weight of many university parapsychologists behind it and could in time turn the whole art of ghost hunting into a quest for unusual ways that the human mind plays tricks on itself. This is not quite the project that most ghost hunters wish to pursue. There is, however, another possible explanation for ghost hunters' relative successes in perceiving phenomena.

If we accept the theories discussed by Colin Wilson that a sense of danger or other type of heightened experience may heighten our abilities to tune into the paranormal, what exactly do you think a ghost hunter experiences by going on a ghost hunt? The very act of ghost hunting itself puts your nerves on edge, and gives you the feeling of being on a unique adventure. If this is not a heightened experience I don't know what is! That being the case, could not the act of ghost hunting itself help trigger (real) ghosts?

As you can see, all of the main theories of the paranormal experience still have tantalising evidence for and against. So our interest cannot yet be destroyed by scientific ridicule. A scientist may disbelieve, that in itself is fine. But the evidence clearly calls for further research to prove his case – not scoffing from the sidelines.

However there is another way in which we could be wasting our time. Can amateur ghost hunters with limited budgets for equipment (and who are often self-taught) hope to provide some objective evidence for others? Even if a ghost hunter avoids the numerous pitfalls and potential bad practices discussed in this book, it has to be remembered that an old, dark manor house (for example) is not a laboratory and any investigation will not be under laboratory conditions. Natural noises will distract the ghost hunter from possible paranormal ones and owners of premises can accidentally disturb any controls (very few owners want to leave during an investigation).

Even if neither of the above happens, scientists can pose the possibility that they might have. In non-laboratory conditions this 'might have' is virtually impossible to disprove. Ghost hunters should not really be trying to be Newton or Einstein – providers of a whole new science of the supernatural. This is not our strength and we would look silly trying to do it. Yet here are two ways in which ghost hunters are extraordinarily useful. Firstly, ghost hunters, by publishing and identifying and giving at least some credibility to unusual phenomena, can succeed in ensuring that the supernatural remains a subject worthy of debate and (perhaps?) is gradually taken more seriously. Secondly, while the evidence produced on a ghost hunt may not be sufficient to prove ghosts to those not on that investigation, it can be very convincing (both for and against) for those who are attending. Now call me selfish if you like, but one of my first concerns is for me to know in my own mind what all of this strange phenomena means, and for that matter whether I continue to exist in some form after death. It would also be nice if others knew as well. If this though is not possible, a personal quest for truth is certainly a very worthy aim.

Even if we do not actually succeed in achieving these aims, ghost hunters have yet another level on which they can justify their interest. I recently asked some ghost hunters for their thoughts, and this additional level of justification can perhaps be summed up by a quote from a reply sent to me by the veteran ghost hunter Peter Underwood:

> I always hoped, during one of the literally hundreds of ghost hunts I organised and supervised over the last sixty years, that irrefutable proof would become evident of something existing after death, but I never found anything lasting. Perhaps we are not meant to find it!
>
> In all my investigations, in all sorts of circumstances and in the company of all sorts of individuals I never encountered anything that proved life after death to my satisfaction. However I have had some truly remarkable and interesting experiences and some wonderful times in some fascinating locations – and I am still hoping!

Perhaps then ghost hunting is not just the thrill of the capture, but the thrill of the chase. Whether your interest is active or purely from books and television, I would hope that this strange fascination in discovering whether ghosts actually exist will continue to thrill us long into the future.

Good ghost hunting!

USEFUL CONTACTS AND SOURCES OF INFORMATION

The Ghost Club
PO Box 160
St Leonards-On-Sea
TN38 8WA
www.ghostclub.org.uk

The Society for Psychical
Research
49 Marloes Road
Kensington
London
W86LA
Tel./Fax: 0207 9378984

ASSAP
27 Old Gloucester Street
London
WC1N 3XX
www.assap.org

The Spiritualist Association
of Great Britain
33 Belgrave Square
London
SW1X 8QB
Tel: 020 7235 3351
www.spiritualistassociation.org.uk

The College of Psychic Studies
16 Queensberry Place
London
SW7 2EB,
Tel: 020 7589 3292/3
www.collegeofpsychicstudies.co.uk

Fortean Times
Tel: 0845 126 1054
www.forteantimes.com

Paranormal Magazine
www.paranormalmagazine.co.uk

Cambridge Ghost Walk
Contact: Alan Murdie
Email: camghost@hotmail.com
Tel: 01284 756717 or 07958
552869

Guildford Ghost Walk
Contact: Philip Hutchinson
Email: philip@ghosttourofguild-
ford.co.uk
Tel: 01483 506232 or (mobile)
07905 288833.
www.ghosttourofguildford.co.uk

The Parapsychological
Association
PO Box 24173
Columbus
OH 43224
USA
www.parapsych.org

The School of Parapsychology
www.theschoolofparapsychology.org

York Ghost Walks
There are numerous different
options, go to www.visityork.org and
choose for yourself!

Skeptics in the Pub
http://skeptic.org.uk/events/
skeptics-in-the pub

The Harry Price website
www.harryprice.co.uk

The Author
jfraserghosthunting@hotmail.co.uk

BIBLIOGRAPHY

Adams, P., Brazil, E., Underwood, P. (2009) *The Borley Rectory Companion* (The History Press)

Alexander, Mark (1975) *Phantom Britain* (Muller)

Alexander, Mark (1981) *Enchanted Britain* (Book Club Associates)

Board, J. & C. (1985) *Alien Animal* (Panther Books)

Fontana, D. & Keen, M. (1999) 'The Scole Report' (The SPR)

Green, A. (1976) *Ghost Hunting: A Practical Guide* (Mayflower Books)

Green, A. (1974) *Our Haunted Kingdom* (Fontana)

Harper, Charles G. (1907) *Haunted Houses* (Reprinted by Senate, 1994)

Hippisley Coxe, Anthony D. (1973) *Haunted Britain* (Hutchinson and Co.)

Hunt, Stoker (1985) *Ouija: The Most Dangerous Game* (Harpur and Row)

Moor, Major Edward (1841) *Bealings Bells* (Reprinted by The Ghost Club, 2004)

O'Keeffe, C. and Roberts, B. (2008) *The Great Paranormal Clash* (Apex Publishing Ltd)

Osborne-Thomason, Natalie (1997) *Walking Through Walls* (Janus Publishing Co.)

Price, Harry (1940) *The Most Haunted House in England* (Reprinted by Time Life Books, 2003)

Raupert, J. Godfrey (1919) *New Black Magic and Truth about the Ouija Board* (Reprinted by Kessinger Publishing)

Thiselton-Dyer, T.F. (1893) *Ghost World* (Reprinted by Senate Press, 2000)

Underwood, Peter (1971) *A Gazeteer of British Ghosts* (Reprinted as *The A-Z of British Ghosts*, Chancellor Press, 1992)

Underwood, Peter (1986) *The Ghost Hunter's Guide* (Blandford Press)

Underwood, Peter (1994) *Nights in Haunted Houses* (Headline Books)

Wilson, Colin (1979) *The Occult* (Grafton Books)

Wilson, Colin (1981) *Poltergeist* (New English Library)

Index

Other titles published by The History Press

The Borley Rectory Companion
PAUL ADAMS, EDDIE BRAZIL AND PETER UNDERWOOD

From 1900 until it burned down in 1939, numerous paranormal phenomena were observed at Borley Rectory. The sightings were a media sensation, and made paranormal investigator Harry Price a household name. This comprehensive guide attempts to establish exactly what went on in 'the most haunted house in England'.

978 0 7509 5067 1

Ghost Hunter's Casebook
BOWEN PEARSE

Andrew Green was one of Britain's most active and best-known ghost-hunters. The Daily Telegraph famously christened him 'the Spectre Inspector'. This is an essential guide to the career of Britain's most famous ghost-hunter, and indeed to the paranormal history of 'our haunted kingdom'

978 0 7524 4500 7

Haunted Guildford
PHILIP HUTCHINSON

From heart-stopping accounts of apparitions and related supernatural phenomena to first-hand encounters with ghouls and spirits, this collection of stories contains new and well-known spooky tales from around Guildford. This selection is sure to appeal to anyone interested in the supernatural history of the area

978 0 7509 3826 9

Haunted Edinburgh
ALAN MURDIE

Containing heart-stopping accounts supernatural phenomena, *Haunted Edinburgh* takes the reader on a tour of the city's streets and buildings, through convents, cellars, churches and attics. Drawing upon the author's own extensive archives it will delight anyone with an interest in the ghostly history of the city.

978 0 7524 4356 0

Visit our website and discover thousands of other History Press books.

www.thehistorypress.co.uk